Yerma

D0318609

Reviews of previous volumes in the series

Bodas de sangre
This excellent edition is ... most welcome. A select bibliography, a brief vocabulary, several footnotes to explain points of difficulty, fourteen long end-notes ... and even the music of the songs, make the edition an extremely valuable and interesting volume, offering the reader the text of the play itself and important new insights into its structure, its significance and indeed its success.   *Modern Languages Review*

Réquiem por un compesino español
This volume will no doubt become the standard text for English readers for some time
Modern Languages Review

This is an excellent edition of *Réquiem*, not least for its thorough and penetrating introductory essay.   *Bulletin of Hispanic Studies*

Será ahora cuando reciba un merecido estudio por parte de Patricia McDermott tras tiempo de espera, y tanto profesores como alumnos debemos sentirnos muy agradecidos por la introducción a la nueva edición del libro por parte de Manchester University Press que nos permitirá adentrarnos en la obra con mayor facilidad.   *Vida Hispánica*

Federico García Lorca

Yerma

edited with introduction, critical analysis, notes and vocabulary by

Robin Warner

Manchester University Press
Manchester and New York

distributed exclusively in the USA and Canada by St Martin's Press

Yerma by Federico García Lorca based on *Obras Completas* (Colección Austral, Espasa
Calpe edition), © 1994 by Herederos de Federico García Lorca. All rights reserved. For
information regarding rights and permissions for works by Federico García Lorca,
please contact William Peter Kosmas, 25 Howitt Road, London NW3 4LT

Published by Manchester University Press
Oxford Road, Manchester M13 9PL, England
and Room 400, 175 Fifth Avenue, New York, NY 10010, USA

Distributed exclusively in the USA and Canada
by St. Martin's Press, Inc., 175 Fifth Avenue, New York, NY 10010, USA

British Library Cataloguing-in-Publication Data
A catalogue record for this book is available from the British Library

Library of Congress Cataloguing-in-Publication Data
García Lorca, Federico, 1898-1936.
      Yerma / García Lorca : edited with introduction, critial analysis, notes, and
   vocabulary by Robin Warner.
         p.   cm. — (Hispanic texts)
      Includes bibliographical references.
      ISBN 0-7190-4131-7 (pbk.)
      I. Warner, Ian Robin, 1940-   . II. Title. III. Series.
   PQ6613.A763Y4 1995
   662'.62—dc20   94-12625

      ISBN 0-7190-4131-7 (paperback)

Reprinted 1999

Typeset in Times
by Koinonia Ltd, Manchester
Printed in Great Britain
by Bell & Bain Ltd, Glasgow

Contents

Preface

Lorca did not prepare a definitive version of *Yerma*. The Losada edition of 1938 was based on an actors' copy. Mario Hernández's edition of 1981 (Alianza), utilized comparison with a different actors' copy to propose a number of corrected readings. Some of these were incorporated in the revised *Obras completas* (Aguilar) of 1986. Subsequently, Miguel García Posada has consulted a Lorca manuscript of the play (dated July 1935) to support a further number of textual variants (Colección Austral). The present text is based on the *Obras completas* version, with the incorporation of some of García Posada's variants. The criteria applied were those of coherence and clarity rather than the support of any particular line of interpretation.

This edition is aimed primarily at sixth-formers and undergraduate students. In response to the current interest in socio-political topics, the introduction is, in large part, devoted to the links between the broad configuration of the play and the major issues of its epoch. More detailed commentary on particular dramatic features of the work can be found in the notes and end-notes.

I should like to express my gratitude to Professor Peter Beardsell, General Editor of Hispanic Texts, for his unfailing help, encouragement and advice, as well as to the staff of Manchester University Press. I am also indebted to Dr Patricia McDermott and Dr Carlos Jérez Farrán for assistance in obtaining material.

1994 R.W.

Introduction

Yerma, completed towards the end of 1934, is the second, and most concentratedly intense of Lorca's celebrated trilogy of rural tragedies.[1] Centred on the frustration and humiliation experienced by a childless wife, the play's intrinsic worth is demonstrated by the fact that subsequent advances in the technological control of conception and improvements in the social status of women have in no way lessened its interest and appeal.[2] Such enduring popularity attests Lorca's success in endowing the play with broadly universal moral and artistic qualities; nevertheless, the partisan passions aroused by the first performances in Madrid and Barcelona indicate that *Yerma* raised issues very relevant to the particular sensibilities and concerns of the audiences of its day.[3] Thus any consideration of the play's overall dramatic design should take into account both Lorca's concept of the theatre as a vehicle of social communication and the nature of cultural politics – and political life in general – in Spain during the nineteen thirties.

Plays and audiences

While, from an early stage in his writing career, Lorca had been attracted to the theatre, and a number of plays had been performed, his reputation at the beginning of 1933 rested largely on his poetry. In that year, however, the critical and commercial success, both in Spain and Argentina, of the rural tragedy, *Bodas de sangre*, meant that, for the first time, he could

---

[1] The term 'trilogy' is used here for convenience of reference rather than with the assumption of a projected continuity in the three plays. The first, *Bodas de sangre* (1933), and the third, *La casa de Bernarda Alba* (1936), have also been edited (by Herbert Ramsden) for Manchester University Press.

[2] The Colección Austral edition of *Yerma*, for instance, has been reprinted (and occasionally revised) almost annually since 1971. In Britain, there have been three major productions of the play, and a Punjabi adaptation.

[3] The somewhat confrontational atmosphere of the Teatro Español on the night of 29 December 1939 and the orchestrated campaign against the play in the right-wing press have been extensively studied by EUTIMIO MARTÍN (see Selected Bibliography, 1985, 1986). The Barcelona production, nine months later, became an occasion for public affirmations of Catalan desire for greater independence and of anti-government feeling in general.

1

undertake a new play with the confidence and authority of an established and acclaimed dramatist. The streamlined configuration of *Yerma*, the economy of means, both in dialogue and staging, with which the central themes are foregrounded,[4] reveals a determination to make few concessions to audiences, to challenge them to respond to the play on its own rigorously artistic terms. Lorca's reported comment, after the Barcelona production, that 'the characters begin to speak, and straightaway the audience realizes that something serious is going to happen, something momentous',[5] seems to reflect his satisfaction with the way the overall tone and style of the play are in keeping with a broader objective, that of countering the Spanish theatre's general lack of seriousness and authority. When interviewed on the eve of the original production of Yerma in Madrid, Lorca had stressed that 'el teatro tiene que ganar, porque la ha perdido, autoridad' (*Obras completas*, III, 614*), but it is significant that his fullest and most carefully considered comments on this topic are to be found in two addresses to audiences comprising stage professionals.[6] On both occasions he reminds them that the dignity of their calling rests on the twin pillars of dedication to artistic standards and responsible service to society. Both ideals are betrayed, he warns, by subservience to exclusively commercial considerations, an approach which perpetuates hackneyed formulas and cheats audiences by pandering to their supposed limitations and prejudices.

Lorca was by no means the only Spanish dramatist of his time to deplore the practices of the established commercial theatre, and to see them as symptomatic of moral and intellectual deficiencies in the nation as a whole. In an epoch in which the theatre enjoyed a much more

[4] The artistic adviser to the company which first staged *Yerma* recalls with admiration that Juan's two sisters stamp their presence on the play 'sin más que atravesar la escena dos o tres veces, hoscas en su silencio, y proferir un grito' (Cipriano Rivas Cherif, *Cómo hacer teatro*, Valencia: Pretextos, 1991, 232). Gwynne Edwards similarly notes that elements of staging are carefully concentrated. Lorca, *Three Plays*, London: Methuen, 1987, 26.

[5] 'comencen a parlar els personatges, i ja tot seguit s'endivina que passarà alguna cosa de seriós, de gran' (from Interview with J. Palau-Fabra, Oct. 1935). See, Federico García Lorca, *Obras Completas*, (ed.) Arturo del Hoyo, Madrid: Aguilar, 1989, vol. III, p. 659. This and subsequent references to Lorca's work in the present edition (other than to *Yerma* and to the interview reproduced in MARTÍN (see Selected Bibliography and fn. [12])) are to the appropriate page number of Volume III in the above edition of *Obras completas*.

[6] 'En el homenaje a Lola Membrives', March 1934, (450-4), and 'Charla sobre teatro', February 1935, (458-61). The latter was on the occasion of a special performance of *Yerma* requested by theatre professionals who were unable to attend the play at normal performance times.

* See note to fn. 5.

2

important place in Spanish social life than it does today,[7] his warning that 'un teatro destrozado ... puede achabacanar y adormecer a una nación entera' (459) echoes the complaint of the major renovating dramatist of the previous generation, Ramón del Valle-Inclán, that 'la vergüenza del teatro es una consecuencia del desastre total de un pueblo, históricamente', and he broadly concurred with the views of his contemporary, Rafael Alberti, who used the first night of his play *El hombre deshabitado* in 1931 to denounce 'la podredumbre de la actual escena española'.[8] What particularly distinguishes Lorca's views is the emphasis he places on the theatre's educative function. The term 'enseñar' frequently appears among the effects he considers good plays should achieve, and in an address preceding a special performance of *Yerma* early in 1935 he explicitly compares audiences to schoolchildren, and the authority a play should command to the respectful attention earned by a stern but fair teacher (614). This is a deceptively simple analogy, however; it is worth considering what should be taught, to whom and by what methods.

First, it is clear that, as well as aiming to raise standards of appreciation among habitual play-goers, Lorca envisaged attracting new types of audiences for serious theatre. Secondly, he did not regard audiences as a socially homogeneous group with given tastes and views, but rather as comprising different classes, types of sensibility and potentials for response. His experience, since 1932, as director of *La Barraca*, a touring university theatre group which often performed in rural areas, had convinced him of the capacity of relatively highbrow pieces, aided by unpretentious but imaginative staging and disciplined teamwork, to hold the absorbed attention of simple country people. In a similar vein, he repeatedly insists that the cheapest seats in the theatre are where the most genuinely appreciative spectators are to be found.[9] Such statements are frequently coupled with expressions of contempt for many wealthier theatre-goers. 'El gran desiquilibrio entre arte y negocio'(452), from which the theatre suffers, arises precisely because the tastes, values and

[7] In the view of Andrés Amorós, *Luces de candilejas: los espectáculos en España, 1898-1939,* Madrid: Espasa Calpe, 1991, 93.

[8] Speaking to provincial journalists in 1933, Lorca described the general state of the Spanish theatre as 'por puercos y para puercos' (531). For the other writers' comments, see also J. Hormigón (ed.), *Valle-Inclán: cronología, escritos dispersos, epistolario,* Madrid: Fundación Banco Exterior, 1987, 549; and Rafael Alberti, *La arboleda perdida* (Barcelona: Bruguera, 1980) 284.

[9] 'Yo arrancaría de los teatros las plateas y los palcos y traería abajo el gallinero. En el teatro hay que dar entrada al público de alpargatas' (560). 'Yo espero para el teatro la llegada de la luz de arriba siempre, del paraíso. En cuanto los de arriba bajen al patio de butacas, todo estará resuelto' (615).

3

behaviour of such patrons are deplorable. They belong, by and large, to a 'burguesía frívola y materializada' (596), a class of people bereft of the capacity to respond to artistic or intellectual stimulus; they are 'los señoritos ... los elegantes, sin nada dentro' (608), who 'no quieren que se les haga pensar sobre ningún tema moral' (614).

While such views reflect broad political sympathies, we should bear in mind that Lorca's aim was a theatre accessible *to* ordinary people rather than specifically *for* them. He comments, in 1927, that *Mariana Pineda* is meant to work at two levels, ('uno ... por el que pueda deslizarse con facilidad la atención de la gente' and another deeper meaning, to which 'sólo llegará una parte de la gente' (491)), revealing a binary strategy of communication which persists into later years. What he terms 'mi teatro físico', including lighting, set design, costume, music, choreographed movements, and what has aptly been called 'the ceremony of articulation' in passages of poetically heightened language,[10] serves to capture the attention and appreciation of those not able to catch deeper nuances of meaning or subtler strokes of characterization embedded in the dialogue.[11] Lorca's remarks on the function of metaphorical language in *Yerma* certainly confirm his concept of two simultaneous but distinct theatrical registers:

> Mi teatro tiene dos planos: una vertiente del poeta, que analiza y hace que sus personajes se encuentren para producir la idea subterránea, que yo doy al 'buen entendedor', y el plano natural de la línea melódica, que toma el publico sencillo para quien mi teatro físico es un gozo, un ejemplo y siempre una enseñanza.[12]

There is no question, of course, of any threat to artistic unity in this apparent dualism, since the two levels complement and reinforce each other. Lorca was, in any case, concerned to achieve a dramatic synthesis of expressive modes, linguistic and non-linguistic, rather than giving any

[10] Tony Harrison, *The Independent*, 23/1/93. It is worth noting that Lorca insisted that, in *Yerma*, 'els actors no parlen amb naturalitat' (650).

[11] Lorca stresses, for instance, the importance of pauses and intonation in conveying the 'calidad mágica' of Calderón's lines of verse to spectators unable to follow the thought expressed in them (534-5), and welcomes the opportunity to include extra music and dances in the 1933 Buenos Aires production of *La zapatera prodigiosa* as a means of ensuring that the audience 'captará perfectamente' the thread of fantasy running through the play (3, 570).

[12] See *Conv.*, 42-3, i.e. in 'Conversación con Federico García Lorca', an interview conducted by Ricardo G. Luengo, Valencia, November 1935, reproduced in MARTÍN, 1989. (See Bibliography, 1989). The insistent repetition, in *Yerma*, of certain images probably stems from Lorca's concern to ensure that no-one in the audience missed the structural importance of the play's central symbols.

priority to the conceptual content of spoken dialogue. We should remain aware, however, within Lorca's notion of educative theatre, of a distinction between provision of cultural experience as something enlightening in itself for the majority of spectators, and the subtle presentation of complex artistic and moral topics for a more receptive minority. The nature of the issues raised in a play such as *Yerma* suggests that Lorca envisaged the perspicacious and thoughtful segment of his audience, intellectually equipped to engage in a socially beneficial process of debate and discussion, the 'público atento que acude con interés al teatro y que después discute apasionadamente, pero con respeto' (636), as belonging to the progressive, educated professional classes, the sector of Spanish society most firmly committed to the reforming and modernizing programme set in train in the first years of the Second Spanish Republic.

Plays and politics

The nature and degree of Lorca's political radicalism, and, in particular, the extent to which it finds expression in his later theatre remains a matter of some disagreement among commentators. As far as his broad stance is concerned, however, it is clear that he supported the modernizing ideals of the Republican–Socialist coalition which came to power in April 1931, on a tide of revulsion against the Monarchy and the corrupt and undemocratic political system it had presided over. There is a persistent strain of criticism, in Lorca's public statements, of certain traditional interests and attitudes which for too long had blocked Spain's way forward. His sense of mission as an artist is in keeping with such sympathies, in that his concern is to encourage and consolidate progressive trends in existing society, rather than to promote a radically different social order. In the rural tragedies Lorca does not challenge accepted definitions of culture, unlike some of his fellow-writers, who commited themselves to solidarity (in the words of one of them) 'con las posibilidades de las masas y en contra de esa pobre tradición cultural de la pequeña burguesía'.[13] He rather seeks to reassert perennial artistic values as an antidote to the values of a commercial theatre which was largely in the hands of conservative interests, and whose trivialized content encouraged complacent acceptance of backward ideas and

[13] The novelist César Arconada, writing in *Octubre*, junio-julio 1933. See Jaime Brihuega, *La vanguardia y la república*, Madrid: Cátedra, 1982, 336. Of Lorca's circle, Alberti and the poet Emilio Prados would certainly have supported such a view.

5

institutions.[14] Such an approach might well strike us as relatively moderate, but, in the highly-charged political atmosphere of the Republic, cultural matters were prone to become an ideological battlefield. Furthermore, it was precisely Lorca's emphasis on the educative function of artistic theatre that aligned him firmly with a specific political programme.

The new regime was aware that, to secure its stability and continuity, it was necessary not only to improve the economic circumstances of the mass of Spanish people, but also to develop civic consciousness and respect for democratic values. The low standard of education and poor conditions of living and working of the populace at large in no way encouraged informed, tolerant social attitudes, but rather had the effect either of confirming narrow traditional loyalties or of enhancing the appeal of movements calling for revolutionary violence.[15] With the long-term aim, among others, of encouraging the growth of a broad sector of popular support, intellectually and morally equipped to resist manipulation from either left or right, the government launched an ambitious programme of educational expansion and reform. The important status this policy accorded to culture as a modernizing and civilizing influence, a means of bringing 'el aliento del progreso' and 'estímulos morales'[16] into the lives of the disadvantaged masses, attracted the support of many artists and writers. Lorca's enthusiastic work with *La Barraca* clearly reflected a desire to help put such a programme into practice.

One inevitable effect of mobilizing culture as an instrument of social change was to blur the distinction between civic and artistic objectives. Lorca's repeated claims for the success of his productions with *La Barraca* among 'el pueblo más pobre y más rudo' (596) seem designed to vindicate government policy as well as his own theories of good theatre. Even the purposeful turn to tragedy initiated with *Bodas de Sangre*, – 'Hay que volver a la tragedia. Nos obliga a ello la tradición de nuestro teatro dramático.' (605) – has a certain ideological significance, since promoting a sense of shared cultural heritage could help to establish a national consensus of values of the sort encouraged by the progressive

[14] There is thus, in my view, a political tinge to the aims of artistic renovation attributed by Andrew A. Anderson to the rural tragedies in 'The Strategy of García Lorca's Dramatic Composition 1930-1936', *Romance Quarterly*, 33 (1986), 211-29, (217).

[15] While some workers affiliated to the Socialist party might be persuaded to collaborate with the reformist aims of the governing coalition, anarchists, both in Cataluña and in the rural south, as well as the growing membership of the communist party, maintained a firmly revolutionary perspective.

[16] See in GIBSON, 1987, 144, Decree of 29 May 1931 setting up the Misiones Pedagógicas.

6

regime. Tragedy, moreover, is a very appropriate vehicle for a serious and stimulating theatre, one capable of strengthening the intellectual and moral resources of a nation entering a new era.[17]

While it was still possible for Lorca to begin serious work on *Yerma*[18] in the optimistic confidence that his artistic ambitions accorded smoothly with official definitions of social usefulness, as well as with a widely-shared desire for orderly progress, the political situation in Spain had changed drastically by the time the play went into rehearsal. Elections in November 1933 had resulted in a conservative government, itself in the shadow of the hard right,[19] and a halt to or reversal of the reforming measures which, in any case, had not been implemented with sufficient effectiveness to keep the Republican–Socialist coalition intact. The hostile suspicion with which liberal intellectuals had been regarded in entrenched but relatively unfashionable conservative quarters had now acquired a measure of official backing. Moreover, the heightening of class tensions during the course of 1934, leading to serious revolutionary insurrections in October and government reprisals on a massive scale, produced an impassioned, sharply polarized political climate. In Spain, as in other parts of Western Europe, the trend to mass mobilization and confrontation was taking over from democratic consensus. Insistence on non-partisan artistic objectivity and universal human values, while useful as a reminder of civilized ideals, was becoming a luxury which writers and artists found increasingly difficult to justify.[20]

Thus, although in the summer of 1933 Lorca could still assert the necessary immunity of artists to 'el morbo político' (530), in the course

[17] A more recent Spanish dramatist (and one similarly interested in the social exemplarity of the tragic *genre*) has insisted on the 'notorias causas sociales' to which Lorca's treatment of moral issues in his rural tragedies draws attention. See A. Buero Vallejo, *Tres maestros ante el público*, Madrid: Alianza, 1973, 154-5.

[18] The idea for *Yerma* may well have germinated earlier, but the work was actually composed during 1933 (in July of that year Lorca announced he was working on a play with the theme of 'la mujer estéril') and 1934.

[19] The largest single party, the Confederación Española de Derechas Autónomas did not, at first, insist on ministerial representation, a decision which reflected its unwillingness to signal acceptance of parliamentary democracy. The tone and scale of the party's rallies were disturbingly reminiscent of the spread of fascism in central Europe during this period.

[20] Shortly before the first performance of *Yerma* Lorca showed a clear awareness of the pressure for choice, however painful, facing liberal intellectuals caught between the alarmingly powerful forces of workers' militancy and fascist reaction: 'Nosotros – me refiero a los hombres de significación intelectual y educados en el ambiente medio de las clases que podemos llamar acomodadas – estamos llamados al sacrificio. Aceptémoslo. En el mundo ya no luchan fuerzas humanas, sino telúricas' (614).

of the following year he repeatedly expressed sympathy with the poor, identified insensitive theatre audiences as the reactionary idle rich, and took pride in his creative activity as conscientious work.[21] While it is true that much of *Yerma* was written under calmer circumstances, Lorca could hardly have been unaware, as he was finishing the play in 1934, that it broached topics – especially the links between definitions of moral standards and the maintenance of traditional social inequalities – that were increasingly tendentious. The 'morales viejas o equívocas' which, according to his 'Charla sobre teatro', it was the task of good theatre to call into question (459), were no longer matters for tolerant debate, but rather touchstones of the conflicts and enmities which divided the nation.

For all the polemic it stirred up in its day, however, we should bear in mind that *Yerma* is not at all the sort of play that is constructed around abstract themes or moral issues. When such topics arise, they do not have an independent status, but are subordinated to an overall artistic design. Matters of moral guilt or responsibility, moreover, so vital for a work's ideological import, are subject, in *Yerma*, to a peremptory tragic determinism. The question, for instance, of who is to blame for the protagonist's failure to conceive is, in one sense, irrelevant. We know from the outset that she will never have a child, because her name is her destiny.[22] Thus, while the element of moral reflection in the play is by no means unimportant, we should appreciate that it emerges through (and its scope is determined by) a dramatic structure geared to a richer and more complex concept of theatre.

Plot-structure and character

The play's subtitle, 'tragic poem', together with Lorca's repeated claim that *Yerma* did not have a plot,[23] suggest a clear intention to concentrate on an essentially unchanging situation and on the inner experience of a

---

[21] A point made by Francisco Caudet in, 'Lorca: por una estética popular (1929-1936)', *Cuadernos Hispanoamericanos*, 433-6 (1986), 763-78, (774).

[22] The protagonist's name is such an unusual one – in its masculine form it denotes a patch of uncultivated land – that, if the other characters frequently addressed her as 'Yerma', her determined refusal to accept that she is, by name and by nature, barren, would seem unconvincing. Consequently, her name is not used until the conclusion of the second act, and her condition is described by terms such as 'seca' and 'marchita'.

[23] In interviews on the occasion of the Barcelona production in September 1935. Lorca insists that 'no hay argumento en *Yerma*', suggesting, in its place, tragic action or theme, or the development of the protagonist's character (650, 651).

central character whose external role is largely passive.[24] Thus the play has a simple story-line, charting the mounting anguish, over a period of some five years, of a childless young country wife. For Yerma, maternity is the consuming purpose of her life, yet she is irrevocably committed to her marriage as the only acceptable means to fulfilling it. Troubled by a sense of something wrong in her relationship with her husband (the hardworking but emotionally withdrawn Juan) she nevertheless refuses to acknowledge her long-standing attraction to Víctor, a local shepherd. Her restless behaviour makes her the object of local gossip and her husband's resentment and vigilance. Víctor leaves the locality and Yerma, increasingly desperate, turns to superstitious remedies, further estranging her husband. When finally, during the course of a pilgrimage that is a barely christianized fertility rite, Juan admits he has neither wanted a child nor cared about her unhappiness, Yerma kills him, embracing despair as an end to the torment of waiting and hoping.

This minimal course of events unfolds through a carefully stylized dramatic structure, a sequence of six scenes in which development of the action is embedded in various effects of repetition. Insistent metaphors of water and thirst, growth and desiccation, often deployed in the more memorable setting of verse, convey the increasing intensity of the protagonist's obsession and, in the play's two large-scale ritual sequences, provide a counterpoint of joyful fecundity to her sad emptiness. Diurnal and, to a lesser extent, seasonal cycles and the social activities and customs associated with them are frequently evoked, and there is a contrasting pattern of indoor and outdoor settings. Where interaction between characters is concerned, there is a marked tendency to echo previous episodes. The exchanges between Yerma and her husband are progressively more confrontational, but spiral inevitably through what are essentially the same pleas, reproaches and failures of understanding. A number of dialogues between Yerma and relatively minor characters centre around giving or requesting advice and defining an overall outlook on life. Her three encounters with Víctor each follow a similar pattern of small talk accompanied by silences and gestures which betray a far more than polite interest, but, on each occasion, the threshold of openly acknowledging feelings remains uncrossed.

Nevertheless, rather than regarding *Yerma* as a play which dispenses with plot, it would be truer to say that the normal dramatic function of complicating intrigue is conspicuously undermined. When he described

[24] Lorca's brother, a perceptive analyst of the plays, comments that: 'in *Yerma* nothing really happens. Everything happens *to* the protagonist, around whom the tragedy revolves'. See FRANCISCO GARCÍA LORCA 1989, 211.

the impression of plot development given at certain junctures as 'a little deception',[25] Lorca was probably alluding to the way conventional expectations are raised, only to be defeated or subverted. To present, as *Yerma* does, a husband-wife-other man triangle, and link it to notions of honour endangered by public gossip, is to provide the basic ingredients for plot lines very familiar to Spanish audiences, not only from Golden Age 'dramas de honor', but also from treatments of marital betrayal and revenge in well-known nineteenth century melodramas. The outcomes, however, are anything but predictable. Yerma escapes from jealous vigilance seeking not the arms of a lover but aids to fulfilment in those of her husband. Víctor, the potential means (but never the actual occasion) of transgression, is simply removed from the scene. At the play's climax, it is not the suspect wife who lies dead on the stage, victim of an extreme but justified fit of passion, but the suspicious husband. While the action of *Yerma* pointedly fails to develop along traditional lines suggested by the central situation, it equally avoids the familiar schema of the European realist theatre, in which a central character's personal unhappiness or frustration (as in, say, Ibsen's *A Doll's House*) leads to heightened critical insight into and decisive rejection of oppressive social values.[26] The idea of leaving her husband is completely repugnant to Yerma, and although she does come to a deeper knowledge of her life's meaning, it is on a purely existential plane, perceiving herself as the victim of an implacable destiny rather than constricting social attitudes and institutions.

Lorca's overall approach to the theatre was, in any case, one which aimed to transcend the limitations of realism. Ultimately, his avoidance of intrigue in *Yerma* probably reflects Lorca's concern to maximize the play's aesthetic and emotional impact as an evocation of the mood of classical tragedy. His pride in this aspect of the work is attested in a number of reported comments, most of which link the absence of plot to the prominent role of choruses as providers of commentary on the unchanging theme of the tragedy, the intensifying plight of a protagonist who represents 'la imagen de la fecundidad castigada a la esterilidad' (616).[27] The action thus develops through a series of contrasts between 'lo estéril y lo vivicante' (617) rather than through a causal chain of events.

---

[25] 'Repeteixo que *Yerma*, d'argument no en té. En molts moments, el públic li semblarà que n'hi ha, pero és un petit engany' (650).

[26] See *Conv.*, 43. Lorca noted with satisfaction that one observer had likened the polemical reaction to *Yerma* to that provoked in its day by *A Doll's House*.

[27] Lorca generally uses the term 'tragedia' to refer to the overall dramatic structure of *Yerma*. He seems perhaps more concerned to evoke patterns of ancient ritual and create a distinctive tragic mood rather than to follow the precepts of classical tragedy.

The large-scale choral sequences, such as the scene of the village women washing clothes in the stream and the mating ritual of the closing scene, with their celebration of instinctive erotic attraction and the fecundity of nature, vividly confirm Yerma's grounds for unhappiness, emphasizing her embittered sense of exclusion from life's underlying purpose. Such sequences tend to hold the action in a frame and enrich its significance rather than move it forward.[28]

On the other hand, while Yerma is a relatively passive figure where external action is concerned, she is clearly the instigator of the inner action, which could be described as a search for the solution to the puzzle of her continued failure to conceive a child. When the answer is revealed to her, it comes as a genuine tragic recognition of the truth: 'Desde que me casé estoy dándole vueltas a esta palabra, pero es la primera vez que la oigo, la primera vez que me la dicen en la cara. La primera vez que veo que es verdad' (3, 2).[29] In *Yerma* Lorca is undoubtedly successful in achieving tragic intensity and coherence by largely abandoning the structural support of a conventional plot in favour of a synthesis of evocative plastic effects, rhythmic alternations of mood, and the powerfully imaginative expression of basic human emotions. In the absence of distractive complications of action, our attention is directed firmly to the figure of the heroine, whose growth in tragic stature derives not from a reaction to calamitous events, but from the courage of her response to a progressively more unbearable situation.

So dominating is Yerma's presence that other characters tend to serve as foils for different sides of her dramatic personality. Even her husband is progressively revealed as a distorted reflection of her cares and obsessions. He too, we learn, resents being cheated of the normal satisfactions of married life, feels threatened by the naming of unpalatable truths, is driven by his worries to spend sleepless nights, regrets he cannot live up to the role expected of his sex, and perceives inanimate nature as an accusing reminder of his sense of inadequacy. Yet his concerns shrink into pettiness when matched against the scale of Yerma's tribulations and the insistence with which they are brought to our attention. Other characters may come

---

[28] The scene of the village women washing does, of course, impart some new information—that Yerma's odd behaviour and gossip about her alleged flirting with Víctor has led her husband to set his unmarried sisters to watch over her. The bulk of the scene, however, is devoted to thematic underpinning.

[29] Yerma effectively acknowledges her symbolic name. There are parallels here with Oedipus, who finally realizes that his name ('clubfoot') holds the clue to his concealed parentage and the identity of his father's murderer. Similarities between the tragic evolution of Yerma and Oedipus were first pointed out in Calvin Cannon, '*Yerma* as Tragedy', *Symposium*, 16 (1962), 85-93.

and go, but, with the exception of the third scene, the figure of the protagonist is constantly before us. So strong a focus on one character inevitably has the effect of placing her mode of being, her feelings, beliefs and motives, at the centre of the play's significance. Such concentration also has the effect, perhaps, of loading Yerma's dramatic characterization with a wealth of complexity which can come close to ambivalence where the audience's empathy with the heroine's scale of values is concerned.

We could imagine, for instance, a different version of the play, one in which the heroine's struggle was purely to come to terms with her inexplicably but irremediably blighted life. Instead, more ambitiously, Lorca gives Yerma's plight the characteristics of a moral dilemma. Childless, she feels humiliated and worthless, but the remedy (opting for a more potent and arousing partner) would equally entail a complete loss of self-respect. Yerma's determination to keep faith with herself, turning her face against any vicarious solution to the suffering that is uniquely hers, undoubtedly enhances her tragic standing. At the same time, however, it emphasizes her belief in inhibition and submission (expressed in notions of honour, decency and duty) as the essence of virtuous conduct.[30] While such values are largely endorsed by the community depicted in the play, this is not invariably the case where the theatre audience is concerned. In spite of the temptation to respond with uncomplicated enthusiasm to a worthy addition to the Spanish stage's long line of vehemently honourable heroines, many spectators might well be inclined to view Yerma's convictions as ideological supports of a backward and, especially for women, repressive social order. Thus, when the protagonist affirms her moral integrity in terms of unswerving conformism to pre-imposed definitions, as she does, for instance, in her scornful rejection of a liaison with the Vieja Pagana's son,

Yo no puedo ir a buscar. ¿Te figuras que puedo conocer otro hombre? ¿Dónde pones mi honra? El agua no se puede volver atrás, ni la luna llena sale al mediodía. Vete. Por el camino que voy seguiré. ¿Has pensado en serio que yo me pueda doblar a otro hombre? ¿Que yo vaya a pedirle lo que es mío como una esclava? (3, 2)

there is a risk of eliciting two different and possibly contradictory modes of response: awe at a tragic heroine bent on pursuing her demand for justice against an implacable destiny through to the end; and sympathy for

[30] Yerma's 'honra' – 'la honra españolísima' as Lorca ironically referred to it (*Conv.*, 42) – while concerned with matters of marital fidelity and the opinion of others, is essentially, for women, pride in honouring a personal commitment to be bound by the rules. Self-esteem is thus self-control. For a useful summary of Lorca's approach to the honour tradition in the Spanish theatre, see LYON 1987, 42-4.

a hapless captive of the traditional moral indoctrination that equates personal fulfilment or pride with self-denial and conformity to fixed patterns of behaviour.[31] We should not assume, moreover, that such uncertainty, is limited to audiences of our own time, more attuned to issues of gender-oppression and ideological conditioning in general. Such matters were particularly topical in Spain during the thirties, and many spectators of Lorca's day would have been ready not only to question the values Yerma so stoutly defends, but also to assume that the play invited them to do so. On the other hand, while we might wonder whether Yerma can simultaneously be for us a victim of tragic forces and a neurotic product of repressive social attitudes, it is worth bearing in mind that Lorca was aiming at a synthesis of classically tragic and modern effects. The classical theme of the barren woman, he announced in July 1934, was to be treated with 'un desarrollo y una intención nuevos' (605). We should also remember, of course, that *Yerma* is not a narrowly cerebral play, but one that works in performance through a powerful – and subtle – theatrical physicality and sensuously emotional language, rather than through the interplay of ideas. While the play does contain elements of social criticism, the different ideological persectives presented seem too contradictory in important respects to justify interpreting it as a work of protest, or as a wholly cogent advocation of a more rational and just ordering of society. On the other hand, to regard the play as essentially apolitical is to miss the controversial significance of its content for audiences of the day. It is useful, at this point, to give some attention to the broader cultural and historical circumstances of *Yerma*'s production.

Yerma and contemporary social issues

The hostile reaction provoked by *Yerma* in right-wing quarters can be partly attributed to the well-known political sympathies of the actress who took the title role,[32] but the play's polemical impact probably owes as

[31] Yerma's 'doblar a *otro* hombre' and her unconsciously ironic refusal of servitude (what she means by 'lo mío' is a subordinate domestic role as a rearer of children) anticipates a notorious incident in *La Casa de Bernarda Alba* when Adela, in an apparently fundamental act of rebellion, breaks her domineering mother's stick, only to proudly define her gesture as choice of subservience to her man. It seems likely, in both instances, that Lorca is making a point about the traditional ideological conditioning of women.

[32] See in GIBSON, 389, that the 'Right' considered Margarita Xirgu to be virtually a communist. Her company had become associated with polemical productions (including Alberti's provocative *Fermín Galán* in 1931) and she had publically shown solidarity with Manuel Azaña, the republican former prime minister imprisoned in the aftermath of the October insurrections.

much to the way it raises matters at the heart of the often bitter disputes between reformers and conservatives that dogged the course of the Second Republic. The obviously contentious issues in the play are those of sexual and religious politics, but it is worth noting that it also touches on another raw nerve, conditions of life among the rural populace. Again, while the work avoids overt political tendentiousness, we should appreciate that the mere open acknowledgement of certain 'facts of life', whether physiological or social, is offensive to those who believe (as many entrenched conservatives did in the Spain of Lorca's day) in the maintenance of ignorance and silence as the mainstays of moral standards and the established order.[33] Not only does *Yerma* break taboos of this sort, but the play also suggests that traditional public morality wrecks private lives. Indeed, certain characters, such as the Vieja Pagana, and the Muchacha Segunda put forward the view that personal happiness or peace of mind can only be achieved by disregarding 'respectable' beliefs and standards of behaviour.

At a broader level of meaning, the natural world continually evoked in the play's language, and often foregrounded in the form of animistic rituals, in no way stands for a hierarchically ordered scheme of creation of the sort typically invoked by those who preach obedience to traditional authority. Instead, it represents powerful, instinctive and potentially disruptive forces that the social order can hope to legitimize or channel, but never suppress. The alternation of moralistic censure and celebration of the sexual-procreative urge by the chorus of laundresses well illustrates this tension, as does the uneasy coexistence, in the play's last scene, of devotional and pagan practices. The Church's inability to impose its controlling definitions on beliefs and traditions deeply ingrained in the rural populace is emphasized by the fact that only gullible children regard the masked dancers as 'el diablo y su mujer'. A number of features of Yerma's predicament similarly suggest that all is not well with the established order. Her loveless marriage had been arranged, as was the case for many country girls, to provide economic security, since it is clear that Juan is relatively well-off, whereas Víctor, to whom she has been attracted since adolescence, does not seem economically capable of supporting a wife.[34] The function of traditional customs and beliefs in reinforcing the passive and restricted lives of women is made perfectly clear

[33] Hence the accusations of obscenity levelled at the work by conservative theatre reviewers.

[34] Mary Nash considers that the idea of marriage for love lay beyond the horizons of the majority of Spanish women in this period; girls from a poor background normally married for economic security. See *Mujer, familia y trabajo en España, 1935-1936*, Barcelona: Anthropos, 1983, 22-5.

in the play; indeed, there is a certain grim social determinism in the spectacle of a woman destroyed because she is whole-heartedly committed to subordinate status, but denied the reproductive function which serves to compensate for it. There is, however, some uncertainty as to the scope and degree of social criticism embodied in the dramatic characterization of the protagonist, of a sort which can make the ideological import of the play difficult to interpret. Before taking up this point, it would be as well to survey some issues and arguments to do with sexual politics in Spain during the thirties.

An important overall aim of liberal modernizing policies was to replace unthinking acceptance of traditional rules and roles by a more rational appeciation of the democratic balance between the needs and rights of individuals and those of the community. The measures adopted during the first two years of the Republic to improve the status of women and raise the quality of education were thus complementary aspects of the same bid for hearts and minds. Predictably, there was fierce opposition from the principal defender of traditional values and institutions, the Catholic Church. From the outset, the clergy made no secret of their dislike for the new regime, which, for its own part, incorporated traditions of thought which saw the power and influence of the Church as the major obstacle to progress, and numbered, among its popular support, many who harboured violent anti-clerical attitudes.[35] While the majority of priests and Catholic spokesmen stressed traditional attitudes to women, property, work and the family, and attempted to discredit a democratic constitution that separated Church and State, the government set out to curtail the Church's access to traditional sites of indoctrination. Its influence in schools was attacked through insistence on secular education and attempts to ban religious orders from teaching, while legislation on the vote, divorce, civil marriage, and access to official posts, designed to promote the social emancipation of women, had the useful effect of encouraging the principal shapers of young minds within the family unit to place a higher value on independence of outlook, and thus become less subservient to the instructions of the priesthood.[36]

Such measures, however, were unlikely to have much immediate effect beyond the limited circle of the urban educated classes. Only a handful of women deputies were elected to the Cortes, and the extension

[35] A resentment which found expression in an outbreak of attacks on churches and other religious sites on the arrival of the Republic.

[36] Some measure of Lorca's attitude to the issue of the Church's influence on schooling can be judged from his association with the Residencia de Estudiantes in Madrid, a product of the Institución Libre de Enseñanza, originally set up by liberal intellectuals to introduce modern, lay principles into Spanish education.

of the vote to women was resisted even by some Socialists and Republicans, who were quick, moreover, to blame electoral defeat in 1933 on the conservatism of the mass of new women voters.[37] Lorca was undoubtedly realistic in his depiction of the rural society of *Yerma* as one untouched by the assertion in the 1931 Constitution that 'el matrimonio se funda en la igualdad de derechos para uno y otro sexo' and Yerma herself is clearly unable to view her problems in the light of the legislation of 1932, which provided for divorce 'cuando lo pidan ambos cónyuges de común acuerdo'.[38] A revealing statistic from the period 1931-33 is that, even though many women's petitions for official separation or divorce stemmed from a 'backlog' of already established situations, in Lorca's home province of Granada the total was a mere sixty nine; as a proportion of marriages, this figure corresponded to a twentieth of the rate for Madrid, suggesting a huge gulf in attitudes between the major cities and the rural provinces.[39] Laws are easier to change than deep-rooted beliefs, and it is with untroubled conviction that characters in *Yerma* 'spout lines that reflect the ideas that have kept women from achieving freedom and equality in Spain'.[40]

In any case, the central assumption of *Yerma*, women's vocation of bearing and nurturing children, was not in itself likely to divide opinions, since the figure of 'la mujer madre' as unquestioned norm permeated all shades of opinion. While the Church continued to insist on a restrictive view of women's allotted place in the scheme of things, liberal opinion tended to postulate a necessarily separate role determined by their function as perpetuators of the species,[41] and even a feminist of libertarian views could argue that 'mujer sin hijos es árbol sin fruto, rosal sin rosas'.[42] Nevertheless, while there was some convergence of opinion on this broad

[37] The socialist deputy Margarita Nelken, for instance, opposed the extension of the franchise to women and her colleague Indalecio Prieto described it as 'una puñalada para la República'. See Geraldine Scanlon, *La polémica feminista en la España contemporánea*, Torrejón de Ardoz: Akal, 1986, 278.

[38] Art. 3 of the 1932 Divorce Law included as grounds, conduct 'que produzca tal perturbación en las relaciones matrimoniales que hagan insoportable para el otro cónyuge la continuación de la vida en común'. See in Nash (fn.[34] above), 235,

[39] Calculated from official figures for 1931-33, reproduced in Nash (fn.[34] above), 250-1.

[40] See KLEIN 1991, 88.

[41] Dr Gregorio Marañón's influential *Tres ensayos sobre la vida sexual*, of 1927, takes such a view. For a description of similar attitudes informing different political perspectives, see Aurora Morcillo Gómez, 'Feminismo y lucha política durante la segunda república' in Pilar Folguera (ed.), *El feminismo en España*, Madrid: Editorial Pablo Iglesias, 1988, 57-84, (62-3).

[42] Federica Montseny. See Nash (fn.[34] above), 158.

issue, the debates over legislation on divorce and the vote ensured that the question of women's rights, responsibilities and social status occupied a prominent position in the ideological battles of the period, especially since it contributed pointedly to a more generalized dispute between supporters and opponents of traditional authority. With the coming of the vote, moreover, women were targeted by political organizations of all colours, and to the arguments in parliament and the press were added the well-publicized views of a plethora of women's groups, formed either as sections of political parties, or as a means of promoting broad gender interests outside the factional arena.[43] It was an issue that Yerma, given its subject matter, could not fail to raise in audiences' minds.[44] The play's treatment of it, however, is not without some ambiguities.

Yerma's basic outlook on life, for instance, can seem not simply acquiescent in but positively supportive of traditional prescriptions. She proclaims her marriage utterly sacrosanct, proudly wears the straight–jacket of honour, acknowledges her husband's authority over her life, and longs for the self-effacement of devoted child-care. The immediate motive for her violent final reaction, moreover, seems to be revulsion at the idea of sex for pleasure rather than procreation. Such a description is rather simplistic and exaggerated,[45] but, nevertheless, sufficiently recognizable to give some idea of potential problems for spectators who, while sensing that Yerma is a figure who should command earnest respect, simultaneously feel that her intransigence rests on unquestioning conformism to dubious principles. It is possible, of course, to see her as a character who has 'internalized' repressive ideologies, whose motives and beliefs are inescapably determined by her conservative environment and upbringing, but such an interpretation runs the risk of denying her the capacity of moral choice necessary to a genuinely tragic outcome. When Lorca refers to Yerma's sense of honour as something 'que va disuelto en su sangre',[46] he seems to be evoking an almost instinctual, atavistic trait, an aspect of her fate rather than a product of sustained brain-washing. In any case, as the play moves toward its climax, it tends to leave ideological issues behind rather than bringing them to a conclusion. The more Yerma's struggle intensifies, the more personal and inward it becomes. As her scornful reaction in the final scene makes clear, to a woman bent on wresting a final answer from the enigma of her intimate pain, the merely

[43] See Morcillo Gómez in Folguera (fn.[41] above), 64-5.

[44] Early in 1935 Lorca identified the two issues which predominantly interested theatre-goers as 'el social y el sexual' (*Conv.*, 40).

[45] On the other hand, some aspects of Yerma's conduct clearly flout traditional definitions of wifely submissiveness and obedience. See MARTÍN 1986, 402-10.

[46] See *Conv.*, 42.

17

social code-breaking offered by the Vieja Pagana seems not only inadequate but irrelevant.

The play's social setting is another possible source of ambivalence. From an artistic point of view, the rural backdrop of *Yerma* is highly effective. Not only does it highlight the elemental quality of the heroine's longings, and enable her expression of them to incorporate a powerful range of natural symbols, but it also provides opportunities for deploying the striking plastic effects and rituals which are one of the play's greatest strengths. Nevertheless, in presenting rural conditions of life in an aesthetic or picturesque light (the masked figures of the last scene are described in the stage directions as 'de gran belleza y con un sentido de pura tierra') the play seems to draw a veil over disquieting realities. As one historian has observed, 'no single area of social or ideological confrontation during the 1930s matched in scope or impact the agrarian problem'.[47] Given the work's focus on an emotional relationship, it is not surprising, in itself, that the village life depicted in *Yerma* seems untouched by the sharpening, in the political climate of the Republic, of the divisions and antagonisms caused by the diversity of property relations in rural Spain, or by the frequent outbreaks of violence which, particularly in the south, accompanied the escalating militancy of poor farm workers. On the other hand, to link the protagonist's plight firmly to rural attitudes and patterns of life was inevitably to provide an uncomfortable reminder of the threat to stability posed by conditions of life in the countryside and the social unrest they provoked, a threat, moreover, which was a major topic of debate and public concern.[48] Yet, while the play presents certain conservative rural attitudes as harmful (and therefore in need of reform) it also seems to make the assumption that an essentially timeless peasant ethos is an appropriate metaphor for life's changeless underlying values.

If there is an inconsistency here, it is one deeply rooted in the contradictory ideological currents of the era. Lorca was well aware of the dehumanizing effects of poverty and, after the traumatic events of October 1934, increasingly willing to condemn them openly. At the same time, his attitude reflects an intellectual tendency to admire the values of the rural 'pueblo', especially its traditional language and culture, as an

[47] See Paul Preston 'The Agrarian War in the South' in Paul Preston (ed.), *Revolution and War in Spain, 1931-1939* (London: Methuen, 1984), 159-81 (160).
[48] The withdrawal of socialists from the governing coalition had been provoked largely by the government's failure either to meet the needs and expectations of the rural poor, or to curb the repressive excesses of local officials. The subsequent fall of the liberal regime encouraged a spiteful reimposition of traditional exploitation in rural areas, creating even greater resentment.

abiding source of the nation's strength,[49] and he identifies, as a source of inspiration for his work (with specific mention of *Yerma*) 'la pobreza bienaventurada, simple, humilde, como el pan moreno' (600). It should not surprise us, therefore, that a rural drama evidently concerned with barriers to human freedom and fulfilment should take a relatively neutral stance toward the most basic obstacle of all. It is further worth bearing in mind that liberal, middle-class writers and audiences alike would tend to regard creative production as a sphere of resistance to crude political pressures, rather than a forum for expressing them. A primitive rural setting offered the dramatist a number of advantages, such as earthy directness of feelings, uncluttered moral perspectives and opportunities for heightened expressive effects both in language and in visual composition; to concentrate on such artistic dimensions, largely avoiding the issue of economic hardship, suggests a refusal to accept the stark choice – between defending class privilege or supporting the forces bent on sweeping it away – which was increasingly being thrust upon those Spaniards who favoured moderation and consensual progress. Lorca himself, of course, was to become the most famous victim of this factional intolerance, and the hatreds it engendered, when the inevitable civil war broke out less than two years after *Yerma*'s first performance.

Current meanings

While the ideological thrust of *Yerma* is closely tied to the historical circumstances of its era, the broad issues, especially where the social construction of gender is concerned, continue to have relevance for our own era. On the other hand, it must be admitted that the particular form in which the moral questions posed by the play arise can seem outdated. Rural populations have dwindled, standards of living and education have risen, strict codes of sexual morality have lost their authority, and women not only demand control of their reproductive potential but have access to the technological means to do so. It is worth giving some consideration, therefore, to the qualities which have enabled the play to retain its power to move, fascinate and provoke thought. In stage performance, of course, *Yerma* is one of the most successful examples of Lorca's ambitious concept of poetic theatre, achieving a concerted impact through a carefully orchestrated synthesis of speech, music, gesture, movement, costume, lighting and decor. Quite apart from its high degree of theatrical

[49] Such sentimental solidarity is well summed up by J-C. Mainer: 'lo popular – unos potes de barro, un romance tradicional, un cantar de Lope, una costumbre olvidada – se convirtió para jóvenes y no tan jóvenes en un modo de adhesión emocional al pueblo.' See *La edad de plata (1902-1939)* Madrid: Cátedra, 1981, 289.

effectiveness, however, the play does engage with important aspects of human experience of a kind which transcends the relatively limited relevance of particular themes and settings.

As a number of commentators have pointed out, the elemental emotions and primitive rituals of *Yerma* have a mythical quality, the power to awaken archetypal, deeply human modes of perception and feeling. The intuitions and insights such experiences bring continue to be important to us in spite of having no place (or perhaps precisely because they have no place) in the official orthodoxy of modern rationalism.[50] While happy to accept the praise of specialists who allegedly acknowledged the accuracy of Yerma's characterization in terms of clinical symptoms, Lorca was quick to stress that his intention was not at all to present a case study, but to express primitively powerful emotion, the 'gemido más primario de la naturaleza' (*Conv.*, 41).[51] The same mythical and imaginative qualities, in some recent interpretations, also serve to articulate a protest against authoritarian and life-denying aspects of institutionalized religion.[52] Yet another approach to the play's deeper meanings stresses the suggestive parallels between the situation, both existential and social, of 'la mujer estéril' and that of a gay male, and considers the play as an expression both of Lorca's regret at being biologically excluded from the opportunity for procreative fulfilment and his resentment of the repressive effects of gender stereotyping.[53]

[50] The mythical or archetypal interpretation of Yerma as an embodiment of the ambivalent creative/destructive potential of the Great Mother, put forward in P. L. Sullivan, 'The Mythic Tragedy of Yerma', *Bulletin of Hispanic Studies*, 49 (1972), has received more recent treatment in KNAPP 1987, LIMA 1991, and FEAL 1989. Feal in particular, demonstrates some interesting parallels where this theme is concerned, between Lorca's play and Euripides' *The Bacchae*.

[51] It is precisely because *Yerma* works through imaginative empathy rather than rationalizing explanations that to put forward verifiable 'causes' for the protagonist's condition is to miss the point. Nevertheless, such a view of Lorca's 'intuitive diagnosis', when combined with other, less positivistic approaches, can produce convincing insights into the play. See, e.g., C. B. Morris, 'Lorca's Yerma: Wife Without an Anchor', *Neophilologus*, 55 (1972), 286-97

[52] See, e.g., MARTÍN 1986, MCDERMOTT 1987 and GILMOUR 1992. Lorca's attitude to official religion is not, however, distinctively subversive, but broadly in line with the views of the majority of liberal intellectuals. As a historian of the religious issue remarks, 'from Pérez Galdós to Lorca, Spanish intellectual life was dominated by men the Church could not claim as its own'. See Frances Lannon, 'The Church's crusade against the Republic', in Preston (fn. [47] above), 35-58 (48).

[53] See BINDING 1985. More recently, attention has moved to the problems raised by such an approach, such as how to account for the impression that 'the women in the rural tragedies are portrayed in ways which come uncomfortably close to reconfirming matriarchal priorities' (see SMITH 1989, 118).

It is less contentious and possibly more productive to see the central problematic of the play as one which lies deeper than specific issues of gender or political ideology. Yerma's sense of failure is of a fundamental kind, a drastic form of the frustration felt, to some degree, by any human spirit conscious of the indifferent otherness of a world whose front line of resistance against our needs and desires is located in our own bodies. Yerma's habitual mode of expression, full of vivid sensorial experiences and physical realities, serves to emphasize the painful directness of her encounter with the realization that 'Una cosa es querer con la cabeza ...'. The desire to have a child, moreover, is not a matter of progression toward a fully determined objective so much as an impulse to bring the unformed future into being. As such, it can suggest the enigmatic existential horizon of our lives, the continual momentum toward a mysterious other, which is the lot of human consciousness. Indeed, Yerma's unhappiness can be seen as that of a life which loses its way forward, estranged from the vital flux of becoming so often symbolized, in the play, by flowing water. She finds herself trapped in a world which is a petrified counterpart of her own unyielding obsession, 'como si la luna se buscara ella misma por el cielo' (3, 1). Yerma's insight into the bleak emptiness of her life brings no opportunity, however, for reassessment and self-renewal; when her appeal for strength-giving love and support, 'no me apartes y quiere conmigo', is rejected, she accepts that her fate is sealed: 'Cuando salía por mis claveles me tropecé con el muro. ¡Ay! ¡Ay!. Es en ese muro donde tengo que estrellar mi cabeza!' (3, 1)

If Yerma's particular frustration is relevant to more universally encountered experiences, it is also worth noting that Lorca's handling of it raises another major contemporary concern. In more recent times, the cognitive focus of attempts to understand human experience has moved from interpreting what is described or represented to investigating the processes through which such accounts are produced. While signifying practices or symbolic orders have come to occupy the attention of theorists in the human sciences, imaginative writers have increasingly turned to metafiction, foregrounding not so much an invented world or its hero as the struggle to create meaning, or, more typically, to define the difficulty of such an enterprise. A striking feature of *Yerma* is the way desire to fulfil a physical longing is equated with a search for meaningful self-expression.

Language and meaning

To describe Yerma's need as one of giving meaning to her life is not simply to quibble with existential terminology. Essentially, she strives to bring the imaginary (the child-suffused world of her dreams, reveries, longings) into physical being. It is understandable that she should place so much importance on the human faculty which also effects such a transformation of immanence into presence, the power of utterance. When she pleads 'dejar que de mi cuerpo salga siquiera esta cosa hermosa y que llene el aire' (3. 1), it is clear she regards the ability to utter her feelings as a form of self-affirmation akin to maternal fulfilment, (an experience she consistently imagines as 'hermoso'). Her tendency to speak of – and even to – 'mi hijo', and to use a discourse of presence rather than possibility when talking about maternity, is merely the most noticeable manifestation of a more pervasive trait, one revealed early in the first scene of the play by her verbal enactment of an imaginary nursing of a sick husband, followed by a re-staging of her first confident approach to the bridal bed. Yerma uses language to project herself into a desired role with its appropriate setting, as if words had the power to shape reality into a willed configuration.[54]

Yerma, however, is not alone in such tendencies. Virtually every character in the play treats language as in some way constitutive of reality, and assumes that to speak out and to allow others to do so, or to name names, reveal secrets, offer accounts or explanations, and so on, is to predict and control the direction of lives and the scope of actions. Given such an attitude, it is hardly surprising that problems of communication are common and conversations often develop through one character contesting the appropriateness of what another says. The play, in general, highlights the link between being and speaking not as a smooth transition but as tension and contradiction. The 'crazy' talk of the Second Girl for instance, for all her light-hearted attitude, stems from an uneasy compromise between her desire to be herself and apprehension at the power of normative labelling; eccentricity is safer than open rebellion. The only sustained escape from such tensions comes at points where dialogue, in the normal sense, ceases, that is, in the play's ritual sequences, in which characters have a shared willingness to allow the power of words to submerge individual consciousness in the surging flow of impersonal forces.

At the same time, it should be appreciated that much of the play's reflexive attention to language derives from traditional techniques of handling dialogue. The mainstream Spanish theatre of Lorca's day

[54] In the view of CIFUENTES 1986, 'el espectador … se ve abocado a considerar que no son los hechos sino las palabras lo que rige el curso de la obra', 169. Rupert Allen had touched obliquely on this topic when discussing 'cantar' as an expressive mode. See *Psyche and Symbol in the Theatre of Federico García Lorca*, Austin: University of Texas Press, 1974.

retained a certain taste for melodramatic rhetoric, in the sense not only of giving emotions a full acting-out, but also of using dialogue as an explicit commentary on the emotional and moral meaning of situations and gestures.[55] The following exchange is typical of many in the play, in that drawing attention to the power of words to define and confirm experience is largely a device for explicitly naming characters' feelings and motives:

> YERMA.   ¡María! ¿Por qué pasas tan deprisa por mi puerta?
> MARÍA.   (*Entra con un niño en brazos.*)   Cuando voy con el niño, lo hago. ¡Como siempre lloras!
> YERMA.   Tienes razón. (*Coge el niño y se sienta.*)
> MARÍA.   Me da tristeza que tengas envidia.
> YERMA.   No es envidia lo que tengo; es pobreza.
> MARÍA.   No te quejes.
> YERMA   ¡Cómo no me voy a quejar cuando te veo a ti y a las otras mujeres llenas por dentro de flores, y viéndome yo inútil en medio de tanta hermosura! (2, 2)

Yerma's closing outburst here, however, demonstrates the power of the play's language to transcend such conventional techniques of nomination to achieve more authentic insights and resonances. Her forcefully direct metaphors enact a sense of unique, suffering selfhood, which cannot be reduced to the standard assigned meanings of allocutions and gestures. In a similar way, Yerma's resentment of her inability to be like other women drives her to disparage the discourse of conformity to accepted values, and the maxims and dictums which define a common reality, establish rules and allot roles.[56] She frequently subverts such judgemental definitions by ironically echoing them, exposing them as cruelly irrelevant to her personal feelings and needs. Among many examples of her rejection of normative meanings, one of the most striking is her reply to Dolores' favourable placing of Juan on the conventional scale of marriage partners: '¡Es bueno! ¡Es bueno! ¿Y qué? Ojalá fuera malo.' (3, 1). It is true that Yerma's seditious talk stems from a sense of being unjustly excluded from the pale of conformism, but, nevertheless, in her determination to speak *her* truth, she pointedly challenges the networks of social authority embedded in language.

The treatment of silence is entirely in keeping with the problems of

---

[55] In melodrama, 'not only is the rhetorical mode based on verbal signs that provide a full enunciation of how and what one is, there is also a realm of physical signs that make one legible to others'. See Peter Brooks, *The Melodramatic Imagination*, New Haven: Yale University Press, 1976, 44.

[56] See BERGERO 1988, for a perceptive analysis of the function of such dictums as an enactment of external controls in Lorca's tragedies.

utterance. On one hand, the frequent examples of evasiveness, refusals to speak and demands for silence draw attention to the power of words to flesh out in reality the hazy shapes, desired or feared, that inhabit the limbo of the unspoken. On the other, the silences and pauses, when 'la mirada' takes over from 'la palabra', often convey something very different, the force of deeply buried desires and intuitions that cannot come into consciousness,[57] because, in one of Lorca's most memorable phrases, 'la sangre no tiene voz'.[58] That to speak out is to court the perils of violating a taboo is vividly illustrated by the play's climax. Yerma already realizes that Juan is indifferent to her deepest needs, since she has admitted as much to Dolores; it is his reckless confession that provokes her final desperation, just as it had been the Vieja Pagana's pronouncement that she is 'marchita' that enabled her to recognize the final truth: 'Eso es lo que quería oír de tus labios. No se siente la verdad cuando está dentro de una misma, pero, ¡qué grande y cómo grita cuando se pone fuera y levanta los brazos!'. Shortly after this naming-induced recognition Yerma stops her husband's voice for ever, and explains, with a terrible calm, that she has thus killed her child.

Such a conclusion can only reinforce the deeper resonances of the play's treatment of the obstacles, inhibitions and uncertainties which stand between the creative impulse and its realization. While *Yerma* is by no means a systematic form of metatheatre, a number of elements in the play do evoke some typical themes of the *genre*.[59] It seems possible that the 'idea subterránea' which the action and dialogue are designed to bring out, 'la revelación sutil que sale de la sombra'[60] has to do with the problem

[57] In her account of 'the language of silence' in Lorca's theatre, Dru Dougherty notes in *Yerma* a skilful use of silent pauses to induce audiences to supply the supressed text from their own imagination. See Dru Dougherty, 'El lenguaje del silencio en el teatro de García Lorca', in A. Esteban and J. Étienvre (eds.), *Valoración actual de la obra de García Lorca*, Madrid: Universidad Complutense, 1988, 23-39, 34-5.

[58] See *Conv.*, 40. The phrase is mentioned by Lorca as the title of a projected play on the theme of incest.

[59] Some commentators perceive metatheatrical patterns as present to a greater or lesser extent in all of Lorca's mature plays, rather than being limited to more obvious examples, such as *La zapatera prodigiosa* or deliberately avant-garde works such as *El público*. See, e.g., Rossana Vitale, *El metateatro en la obra de Francisco García Lorca* (Madrid: Pliegos, 1991), who classes Yerma as one of the characters 'cuyas tragedias personales prestan teatralidad a sus vidas', 126.

[60] See *Conv.*, 43. See also LYON 1987, 18-19, such a concept accords perfectly with Lorca's general aim of creating a poetic theatre, in which expression is given to imaginative insights which lie beyond the limited scope of rational–positivist definitions of human experience.

of the subjective self as simultaneously realized through and frustrated by expression. While language is a means of self-realization, it is also a site of repression, whether of social origin (controlling definitions of what counts as authentic or legitimate), or as an embodiment of misrecognitions deeply embedded in human subjectivity. Biological reproduction, moreover, has traditionally supplied a fund of metaphors for artistic creation, the quest to give life and form to obscure feelings and intuitions, to release and communicate what had remained imprisoned in silence. Perhaps the only consoling insight to be derived from the numbing final moment of this 'poema trágico' is that Yerma's path to utter defeat has also been a process of expressive affirmation.

Chronology: Lorca and his epoch

1898 5 June. Federico García Lorca born in Fuente Vaqueros, Granada.
1909 Family moves to the provincial capital.
1915 Attends University of Granada.
1919 Moves to Residencia de Estudiantes, Madrid, a focus for younger Spanish writers, artists and intellectuals.
1920 First play, *El maleficio de la mariposa*, staged in Madrid. Poems begin to appear in literary journals.
1921 *Libro de poemas* published.
1923 General Primo de Rivera seizes power.
1927 *Canciones* (poems 1921-24). *Mariana Pineda* staged by Margarita Xirgu's company in Barcelona and Madrid.
1928 *Primer romancero gitano* published.
1929 Mounting opposition to Primo de Rivera and the Monarchy; in June Lorca leaves Spain to spend a year in USA (Columbia University) and Cuba.
1930 January, Primo de Rivera forced to step down, succeeded by General Berenguer. December, abortive pro-Republican risings, executions, arrests, censorship. *La zapatera prodigiosa* staged in Madrid, again by Margarita Xirgu. *Poeta en Nueva York* and *El público* concluded.
1931 April, Republican victories in local elections, widespread popular demonstrations, Alfonso XIII flees the country. Provisional Republican Government takes power, confirmed in Constituent Elections (June). Majority Socialist–Republican coalition initiates two years of social reform. *Poema del cante jondo* published. *Así que pasen cinco años* concluded.
1932 Lorca helps to organize and begins period as director of state-subsidized travelling university theatre (*La Barraca*).
1933 *Bodas de sangre* successfully staged in Madrid and Barcelona. *Amor de Don Perlimplín* staged in Madrid. October, Lorca leaves for six months stay in Montevideo and Buenos Aires, where *Bodas de Sangre* is rapturously received. Meanwhile, in Spain, elections at the end of the year result in a conservative majority and a halt to liberal reforms.
1934 October, pro-autonomy movement in Cataluña and serious revolu-

tionary insurrection in Asturias. Harsh repression by government and military. Lorca begins to make statements condemning poverty and social injustice. December, *Yerma* staged in Madrid by Margarita Xirgu's company, the first night interrupted by right-wing protests.

1935   May, *Llanto por Ignacio Sánchez Mejías* published. September, Barcelona production of *Yerma*. December, *Doña Rosita* staged in Barcelona. Left parties form a unified Popular Front to contest new elections.

1936   February, Popular Front victory. Worsening of political and social disorder. Lorca completes *La casa de Bernarda Alba* and the poems of *Divan de Tamarit*. July, concerted military insurrection, the start of three years of civil war, finds Lorca in Granada, where the military and their ultra-right allies rapidly take control and launch a ferocious 'cleansing' operation against all suspected dissidents. 19 August, Lorca summarily executed.

Selected bibliography

For more comprehensive bibliographical coverage, see Arturo del Hoyo's 'Bibliografía' in Volume III of Federico García Lorca, *Obras completas* (Madrid: Aguilar, 1986) and the annual 'Bibliografía lorquiana reciente' of Andrew A. Anderson, published in the *Boletín de la Fundación Federico García Lorca* (Madrid). The following items are listed in chronological order. I have judged it more useful to concentrate on post-1980 publications; the major critical contributions to the study of *Yerma* before that date are acknowledged and discussed in many of the items listed below.

1980 Gwynne Edwards, *Lorca. The Theatre Beneath the Sand* (London: Marion Boyars).

Good coverage of *Yerma*'s poetic antecedents, thematic contrasts, and use of stage-settings and dialogue rhythms.

Robert Ter-Horst, 'Nature Against Nature in *Yerma*', in J. W. Zdenek (ed.), *The World of Nature in the Work of Francisco García Lorca*, Winthrop: Winthrop Studies in Modern Writers, 41-51

Sees the play as a symbolic investigation of the affinities between barrenness and fertility in the outlook of the creative artist.

1981 Mario Hernández, Introduction and notes to his edition of *Yerma*, Madrid: Alianza.

Good contextual information and useful compilation of statements by Lorca relevant to the play.

1982 Frances Cate, 'Los motivos de la espera y la esperanza en *Yerma* and *Doña Rosita la soltera*', *García Lorca Review*, 94-113.

Waiting and Hope as universalizing elements.

1983 Hector Romero, 'La frustración de Yerma: un replantamiento', *García Lorca Review*, 203-210.

Emotional and spiritual significance of barrenness.

Julianne Burton, 'The Greatest Punishment: Female and Male in Lorca's Tragedies' in Beth Miller (ed.), *Women in Hispanic Literature. Icons and Fallen Idols*, (Berkeley: University of California, 259-79.

Yerma, like the other heroines, as victim of and rebel against class and gender oppression/exploitation.

Lloyd Halliburton, 'An Aristotelian Analysis of *Yerma*', *García Lorca Review*, 161-169.

Sees a fuller incorporation of the Aristotelian precepts than is usually acknowledged.

1984 Antonio Cao, *Federico García Lorca y las vanguardias: hacia el teatro*, London: Támesis.

Global study of Lorca's imagery, with some useful comments on the dramatic function of images in *Yerma*.

1984   Reed Anderson, *Federico García Lorca*, London: Macmillan.

Concise and perceptive observations on *Yerma*.

1985   Paul Binding, *Lorca: The Gay Imagination*, London: GMP.

Yerma as expression of Lorca's own sexuality – hence its power and complexity.

Gwynne Edwards, *Dramatists in Perspective: Spanish Theatre in the Twentieth Century*, Cardiff: University of Wales.

Tragic mode, stylized structure and language of *Yerma*.

Eutimio Martín, '*Yerma*, o la imperfecta casada' in R. Doménech (ed.), '*La casa de Bernarda Alba*' *y el teatro de García Lorca*, (Madrid: Cátedra, 93-123.

Includes a useful analysis of the hostile reaction to the play in the right wing press.

1986   Andrew A. Anderson, 'The Strategy of García Lorca's Dramatic Composition', *Romance Quarterly*, 33, 211-29.

Useful account of Lorca's overall aims and methods in the rural tragedies.

Ricardo Doménech, 'Realidad y misterio: notas sobre el especio escénico en *Bodas de sangre*, *Yerma* and *La casa de Bernarda Alba*', *Cuadernos Hispanoamericanos*, 433-6, 293-310.

Creation of 'magical' spaces as part of mythical resonance.

Luis Fernández Cifuentes, *García Lorca en el teatro: la norma y la diferencia*, Zaragoza: Universidad de Zaragoza.

Within a useful general approach to Lorca's reworking of stage conventions, analyzes function of language in *Yerma*.

Eutimio Martín, *Federico García Lorca, heterodoxo y mártir*, Madrid: Siglo XXI.

Contemporary right-wing reaction to *Yerma* and the non-conformist characterization of its protagonist.

1987   Ian Gibson, *Federico García Lorca. (2) De Nueva York a Fuente Grande (1929-1936)*, Barcelona: Grijalbo.

Excellent source of biographical and historical details in two volumes, with commentary on the Moclín *romería* and the ideology of honour, vol. 2.

Bettina Knapp, 'Federico García Lorca's *Yerma*: a woman's mystery' in *Women in Twentieth Century Literature*, University Park: Pennsylvania State University Press, 11-23. Also in M. Durán and F. Colecchia (eds.) *Lorca's Legacy*, New York: Lang, 1991, 135-46.

Discerns a pattern of ancient rites and mysteries through which Yerma achieves final liberation.

John Lyon and Jacqueline Minette, General Introduction and Introduction to *Yerma* in the bi-lingual edition of *Yerma*, translated by Jacqueline Minette and Ian Macpherson, Warminster: Aris and Phillips.

Good analysis of thematic and technical trends in Lorca's theatre and of the tragic configuration of *Yerma*.

Patricia McDermott, 'Yerma: Extra Naturam Nulla Salus' in C. A. Longhurst (ed.), *A Face Not Turned to the Wall: Essays on Hispanic Themes for Gareth Alban Davies*, Leeds: University of Leeds, 235-48.

Use of symbolic motifs to suggest alternative cultural patterns and subvert traditional Catholic iconographies/ideologies.

1988   José Alberich, 'Más sobre el teatro de Lorca y Valle-Inclán: variedades del drama rural' in C. B. Morris (ed.), '*Cuando yo me muera*': *Essays in Memory of*

Federico García Lorca, Lanham: University Press of America, 259-76.
Tragic dimensions of rural setting and imagery.

1988   Adriana Bergero, 'Frases hechas y prejuicios para la delimitación del asfixiante espacio de la tragedia' in C. B. Morris (ed.), *'Cuando yo me muera': Essays in Memory of Federico García Lorca*, Lanham: University Press of America, 295-322.

Observations on the language of social control particularly relevant to *Yerma*.

Carlos Feal, 'La idea del honor en las tragedias de Lorca' in C. B. Morris (ed.), *'Cuando yo me muera': Essays in Memory of Federico García Lorca*, Lanham: University Press of America, 277-93.

Contrast of honour and gender psychology in Calderonian and Lorcan tragedies with considerable attention to *Yerma*.

Dru Dougherty, 'El lenguaje del silencio en el teatro de García Lorca' in A. Esteban and J. Étienvre (eds.) *Valoración actual de la obra de García Lorca*, Madrid: Universidad Complutense.

Techniques of silence, most relevant to *Yerma*, some taken from the play.

Guadalupe Martínez Lacalle, 'Yerma: una tragedia pura y simplemente', *Neophilologus*, 72, 227-37.

Lorca's adaptation of classical precepts to create a modern tragedy.

1989   José Ortega, *Conciencia y estética social en la obra de García Lorca*, Granada: Universidad de Granada.

Emphasis on economic circumstances and ideological conditioning as determinants of the tragic outcome.

Carlos Feal, *Lorca: tragedia y mito*, Ottawa: Dovehouse.

Psychomythic structure approach shows parallels with classical treatments of Dionysian themes.

Eutimio Martín, Introduction and notes to his *Antología comentada* of Lorca's theatre and prose, Madrid: Ediciones de la Torre.

Reproduces the important Valencia interview of 15 November 1935.

Linda Materna, 'Los códigos genéricos sexuales y la presentación de la mujer en el teatro de García Lorca' in A. G. Loureiro (ed.), *Estelas, laberintos, nuevas sendas. Unamuno, Valle-Inclán, García Lorca, La Guerra Civil*, Barcelona: Anthropos, 263-77.

Masculine text structure and authorial viewpoint in heroine's characterization.

John Walsh, 'Mujeres en el teatro de Lorca' in A. G. Loureiro (ed.), *Estelas, laberintos, nuevas sendas. Unamuno, Valle-Inclán, García Lorca, La Guerra Civil*, Barcelona: Anthropos, 279-95.

Actresses' dominance of commercial theatre and possible repercussions on the design of plays such as *Yerma*.

Francisco García Lorca, *In the Green Morning. Memories of Federico*, translated by Christopher Maurer, London: Peter Owen.

Perceptive comments on the relations, in *Yerma*, between tragedy and the honour question.

Paul Julian Smith, *The Body Politic. Gender and Sexuality in Spanish and Spanish American Literature*, Oxford: Clarendon.

Includes Foucault-based discussion of language, power and sexuality in the rural trilogy.

1990   Fiona Parker and Terence McMullan, 'Federico García Lorca's *Yerma* and the World of Work', *Neophilologus*, 74, 58-69.

30

Contrast of work-patterns underlying social definitions of women's status.
1991   Miguel García Posada, Introduction and textual notes to his manuscript-based edition of *Yerma*, Madrid: Espasa-Calpe.

Wide-ranging overview of issues raised by the play.

Arturo Jiménez-Vera, 'The Role of Spanish Society in *Yerma*' in M. Durán and F. Colecchia (eds.) *Lorca's Legacy*, New York: Lang, 147-56.

Social criticism expressed in subtle, implicit ways.

Roberto Lima, 'Toward the Dionysiac: Pagan elements and Rites in *Yerma*' in M. Durán and F. Colecchia (eds.) *Lorca's Legacy*, New York: Lang, 115-34.

Complements Feal's demonstration of parallels with the tragic ritual violence of *The Bacchae*.

Dennis A. Klein, *Blood Wedding, Yerma and The House of Bernarda Alba. García Lorca's Tragic Trilogy*, Boston, Twayne, 1991.

Structures, characters, themes, techniques, aimed at a readership unfamiliar with Spanish language and culture.

Andy Piasecki (ed.), *File on Lorca*, London: Methuen.

Selection of reviews, some of English productions.
1992   John Gilmour, 'The Cross of Pain and Death: Religion in the Rural Tragedies' in R. Havard (ed.), *Lorca, Poet and Playwright: Essays in Honour of J. M. Aguirre*, Cardiff: University of Wales, 133-55.

Yerma's subservience to traditional religious morality as a reflection of Lorca's anti-Church stance.

Yerma
*Poema trágico en tres actos
y seis cuadros*

PERSONAJES

YERMA	HEMBRA
MARÍA	CUÑADA 1.ª
VIEJA PAGANA	CUÑADA 2.ª
DOLORES	MUJER 1.ª
LAVANDERA 1.ª	MUJER 2.ª
LAVANDERA 2.ª	NIÑOS
LAVANDERA 3.ª	JUAN
LAVANDERA 4.ª	VÍCTOR
LAVANDERA 5.ª	MACHO
LAVANDERA 6.ª	HOMBRE 1.º
MUCHACHA 1.ª	HOMBRE 2.º
MUCHACHA 2.ª	HOMBRE 3.º

Acto Primero

CUADRO PRIMERO

Al levantarse el telón está YERMA *dormida con un tabaque de costura a los pies. La escena tiene una extraña luz de sueño. Un* PASTOR *sale de puntillas, mirando fijamente a* YERMA. *Lleva de la mano a un* NIÑO *vestido de blanco. Suena el reloj. Cuando sale el* PASTOR,[1] *la luz azul se cambia por una alegre luz de mañana de primavera.* YERMA *se despierta.*[2]

CANTO. (*Voz dentro.*)
> A la nana, nana, nana,[3]
> a la nanita le haremos
> una chocita en el campo
> y en ella nos meteremos.

YERMA. Juan. ¿Me oyes? Juan.

JUAN. Voy.

YERMA. Ya es la hora.

JUAN. ¿Pasaron las yuntas?

YERMA. Ya pasaron.[4]

JUAN. Hasta luego. (*Va a salir.*)

YERMA. ¿No tomas un vaso de leche?

JUAN. ¿Para qué?[5]

---

[1] See Endnote **A**.

[2] Apart from the symbolic meaning of its content, we might note that this silent dream, a prelude to the play's action, is the only time Yerma shows untroubled contentment. She wakes, begins to speak, and her anxieties begin to show themselves.

[3] 'Nana' means both 'baby girl' and 'lullaby'. The song here is a traditional one, singled out by Lorca in a lecture on lullabies as expressing the protective intimacy and reclusion of mother and baby against a threatening world (292). (See note to fn. [5], p. 2.)

[4] i.e. The day's work in the fields is beginning.

[5] This simple exchange hints at depths of incompatibility. Juan snubs a (perhaps not so simple) gesture of care and affection by asking what practical purpose it can serve.

YERMA. Trabajas mucho y no tienes tú cuerpo para resistir los trabajos.

JUAN. Cuando los hombres se quedan enjutos se ponen fuertes, como el acero.

YERMA. Pero tú no. Cuando nos casamos eras otro. Ahora tienes la cara blanca como si no te diera en ella el sol A mí me gustaría que fueras al río y nadaras, y que te subieras al tejado cuando la lluvia cala nuestra vivienda.[6] Veinticuatro meses llevamos casados y tú cada vez más triste, más enjuto, como si crecieras al revés.

JUAN. ¿Has acabado?

YERMA. (*Levantándose.*) No lo tomes a mal. Si yo estuviera enferma me gustaría que tú me cuidases. «Mi mujer está enferma: voy a matar este cordero para hacerle un buen guiso de carne. Mi mujer está enferma: voy a guardar esta enjundia de gallina para aliviar su pecho; voy a llevarle esta piel de oveja para guardar sus pies de la nieve.» Así soy yo. Por eso te cuido.

JUAN. Y yo te lo agradezco.

YERMA. Pero no te dejas cuidar.

JUAN. Es que no tengo nada. Todas esas cosas son suposiciones tuyas. Trabajo mucho. Cada año seré más viejo.

YERMA. Cada año … Tú y yo seguimos aquí cada año …

JUAN. (*Sonriente.*) Naturalmente. Y bien sosegados. Las cosas de la labor van bien, no tenemos hijos que gasten.

YERMA. No tenemos hijos… ¡Juan!

JUAN. Dime.

YERMA. ¿Es que yo no te quiero a ti?

JUAN. Me quieres.

YERMA. Yo conozco muchachas que han temblado y que lloraron antes de entrar en la cama con sus maridos. ¿Lloré yo la primera vez que me acosté contigo? ¿No cantaba al levantar los embozos

[6] See Endnote **B**.

de holanda? ¿Y no te dije: «¡Cómo huelen a manzana estas ropas!»?

JUAN.   ¡Eso dijiste!

YERMA.   Mi madre lloró porque no sentí separarme de ella. Y era verdad! Nadie se casó con más alegría. Y sin embargo…

JUAN.   Calla. Demasiado trabajo tengo yo con oír en todo momento …

YERMA.   No. No me repitas lo que dicen.[7] Yo veo por mis ojos que eso no puede ser… A fuerza de caer la lluvia sobre las piedras éstas se ablandan y hacen crecer jaramagos, que las gentes dicen que no sirven para nada. Los jaramagos no sirven para nada, pero yo bien los veo mover sus flores amarillas en el aire.

JUAN.   ¡Hay que esperar!

YERMA.   ¡Sí, queriendo![8] (YERMA *abraza y besa al marido, tomando ella la iniciativa.*)

JUAN.   Si necesitas algo me lo dices y lo traeré. Ya sabes que no me gusta que salgas.

YERMA.   Nunca salgo.

JUAN.   Estás mejor aquí.

YERMA.   Sí

JUAN.   La calle es para la gente desocupada.

YERMA. (*Sombría.*)   Claro.[9]

(*El marido sale y* YERMA *se dirige a la costura, se pasa la mano por el vientre, alza los brazos en un hermoso bostezo y se sienta a coser.*)

¿De dónde vienes, amor, mi niño?

---

[7] It is worth noting that the first reference to the dangerous authority of words has to do with stigmatizing Yerma as barren rather than indecently flirtatious – although her husband almost immediately shows his characteristic touchiness about the second possibility.

[8] i.e. wanting a child. A first hint of Yerma's obsessional belief in the power of willing and wanting to bring about what is desired.

[9] *Exactly!* (See Endnote C).

«De la cresta del duro frío.»
¿Qué necesitas, amor, mi niño?
«La tibia tela de tu vestido.»

(*Enhebra la aguja.*)

¡Que se agiten las ramas al sol
y salten las fuentes alrededor!

(*Como si hablara con un niño.*)

En el patio ladra el perro
en los árboles canta el viento.
Los bueyes mugen al boyero
y la luna me riza los cabellos.
¿Qué pides, niño, desde tan lejos?

(*Pausa.*)

«Los blancos montes que hay en tu pecho.»
¡Que se agiten las ramas al sol
y salten las fuentes alrededor!

(*Cosiendo.*)

Te diré, niño mío, que sí.
Tronchada y rota soy para ti.
¡Cómo me duele esta cintura
donde tendrás primera cuna!
¿Cuándo, mi niño, vas a venir?

(*Pausa.*)

«Cuando tu carne huela a jazmín.»
¡Que se agiten las ramas al sol
y salten las fuentes alrededor!

(YERMA *queda cantando. Por la puerta entra* MARÍA, *que viene con un lío de ropa.*)

¿De dónde vienes?

MARÍA.   De la tienda.

YERMA.   ¿De la tienda tan temprano?

MARÍA.   Por mi gusto hubiera esperado en la puerta a que abrieran.

38

¿Y a que no sabes lo que he comprado?[10]

YERMA.   Habrás comprado café para el desayuno, azúcar, los panes.

MARÍA.   No. He comprado encajes, tres varas de hilo, cintas y lanas de color para hacer madroños. El dinero lo tenía mi marido y me lo ha dado él mismo.

YERMA.   Te vas a hacer una blusa.

MARÍA.   No. Es porque… ¿sabes?

YERMA.   ¿Qué?

MARÍA.   Porque ¡ya ha llegado! (*Queda con la cabeza baja.*)

(YERMA *se levanta y queda mirándola con admiración.*)

YERMA.   ¡A los cinco meses!

MARÍA.   Sí

YERMA.   ¿Te has dado cuenta de ello?

MARÍA.   Naturalmente.

YERMA. (*Con curiosidad.*)   ¿Y qué sientes?

MARÍA.   No sé. (*Pausa.*) Angustia.

YERMA.   Angustia. (*Agarrada a ella.*) Pero… ¿cuándo llegó? Dime… Tú estabas descuidada…

MARÍA.   Sí, descuidada…

YERMA.   Estarías cantando, ¿verdad? Yo canto. ¿Tú?…, dime.

MARÍA.   No me preguntes. ¿No has tenido nunca un pájaro vivo apretado en la mano?

YERMA.   Sí.

MARÍA.   Pues lo mismo…, pero por dentro de la sangre.

YERMA.   ¡Qué hermosura! (*La mira extraviada.*)

MARÍA.   Estoy aturdida. No sé nada.

YERMA.   ¿De qué?

[10] *I bet you can't guess what I've bought.*

39

MARÍA.   De lo que tengo que hacer. Le preguntaré a mi madre.

YERMA.   ¿Para qué? Ya está vieja y habrá olvidado estas cosas. No andes mucho y cuando respires respira tan suave como si tuvieras una rosa entre los dientes.

YERMA.   Oye, dicen que más adelante te empuja suavemente con las piernecitas.

YERMA.   Y entonces es cuando se le quiere más, cuando se dice ya: ¡mi hijo!

MARÍA.   En medio de todo tengo vergüenza.

YERMA.   ¿Qué ha dicho tu marido?

MARÍA.   Nada.

YERMA.   ¿Te quiere mucho?

MARÍA.   No me lo dice, pero se pone junto a mí y sus ojos tiemblan como dos hojas verdes.

YERMA.   ¿Sabía él que tú…?

MARÍA.   Sí

YERMA.   ¿Y por qué lo sabía?

MARÍA.   No sé. Pero la noche que nos casamos me lo decía constantemente con su boca puesta en mi mejilla, tanto que a mí me parece que mi niño es un palomo de lumbre que él me deslizó por la oreja.[11]

YERMA.   ¡Dichosa!

MARÍA.   Pero tú estás más enterada de esto que yo.

YERMA.   ¿De qué me sirve?

MARÍA.   ¡Es verdad! ¿Por qué será eso? De todas las novias de tu tiempo tú eres la única…

YERMA.   Es así. Claro que todavía es tiempo. Elena tardó tres años, y otras antiguas, del tiempo de mi madre, mucho más, pero dos años y veinte días,[12] como yo, es demasiado esperar. Pienso que

[11] There is a parallel with the Annunciation here, including the name of the mother.
[12] Yerma's exact calculation is eloquent of her single-minded preoccupation.

no es justo que yo me consuma aquí. Muchas veces salgo descalza al patio para pisar la tierra, no sé por qué. Si sigo así, acabaré volviéndome mala.

MARÍA. ¡Pero ven acá, criatura! Hablas como si fueras una vieja. ¡Qué digo! Nadie puede quejarse de estas cosas. Una hermana de mi madre lo tuvo a los catorce años ¡y si vieras qué hermosura de niño!

YERMA. (*Con ansiedad.*) ¿Qué hacía?

MARÍA. Lloraba como un torito, con la fuerza de mil cigarras cantando a la vez, y nos orinaba y nos tiraba de las trenzas y, cuando tuvo cuatro meses, nos llenaba la cara de arañazos.

YERMA. (*Riendo.*) Pero esas cosas no duelen.

MARÍA. Te diré…

YERMA. ¡Bah! Yo he visto a mi hermana dar de mamar a su niño con el pecho lleno de grietas y le producía un gran dolor, pero era un dolor fresco, bueno, necesario para la salud.

MARÍA. Dicen que con los hijos se sufre mucho.

YERMA. Mentira. Eso lo dicen las madres débiles, las quejumbrosas. ¿Para qué los tienen? Tener un hijo no es tener un ramo de rosas. Hemos de sufrir para verlos crecer. Yo pienso que se nos va la mitad de nuestra sangre.[13] Pero esto es bueno, sano, hermoso. Cada mujer tiene sangre para cuatro o cinco hijos, y cuando no los tienen se les vuelve veneno, como me va a pasar a mí.

MARÍA. No sé lo que tengo.

YERMA. Siempre oí decir que las primerizas tienen susto.

MARÍA. (*Tímida.*) Veremos… Como tú coses tan bien…

YERMA. (*Cogiendo el lío.*) Trae. Te cortaré los trajecitos. ¿Y esto?

MARÍA. Son los pañales.

YERMA. Bien. (*Se sienta.*)

---

[13] *we lose half our blood.*

MARÍA.   Entonces… Hasta luego.

(*Se acerca y* YERMA *le coge amorosamente el vientre con las manos.*)

YERMA.   No corras por las piedras de la calle.

MARÍA.   Adiós. (*La besa. Sale.*)

YERMA.   ¡Vuelve pronto! (YERMA *queda en la misma actitud que al principio. Coge las tijeras y empieza a cortar. Sale* VÍCTOR.) Adiós, Víctor.

VÍCTOR. (*Es profundo y lleno de firme gravedad.*)   ¿Y Juan?

YERMA.   En el campo.

VÍCTOR.   ¿Qué coses?

YERMA.   Corto unos pañales.

VÍCTOR. (*Sonriente.*)   ¡Vamos!

YERMA. (*Ríe.*)   Los voy a rodear de encajes.

VÍCTOR.   Si es niña le pondrás tu nombre.[14]

YERMA. (*Temblando.*)   ¿Cómo?…

VÍCTOR.   Me alegro por ti.

YERMA. (*Casi ahogada.*)   No…, no son para mí. Son para el hijo de María.

VÍCTOR.   Bueno, pues a ver si con el ejemplo te animas.[15] En esta casa hace falta un niño.

YERMA. (*Con angustia.*)   Hace falta.

VÍCTOR.   Pues adelante. Dile a tu marido que piense menos en el trabajo. Quiere juntar dinero y lo juntará, pero ¿a quién lo va a dejar cuando se muera? Yo me voy con las ovejas. Dile a Juan que recoja las dos que me compró.[16] Y en cuanto a lo otro…,

[14] In view of the symbolic significance of the heroine's name, Victor's remark can only emphasize how mistaken his supposition is.

[15] *Let's see if she inspires you (to become pregnant).*

[16] As the play progresses, Yerma's growing desperation is accompanied by further allusions to Juan's material success, particularly at the expense of his 'rival'.

42

¡que ahonde!¹⁷ (*Se va sonriente.*)

YERMA. (*Con pasión.*)   ¡Eso! ¡Que ahonde!

(YERMA, *que en actitud pensativa se levanta y acude al sitio donde ha estado* VÍCTOR *y respira fuertemente como si aspirara aire de montaña, después va al otro lado de la habitación, como buscando algo, y de allí vuelve a sentarse y coge otra vez la costura. Comienza a coser y queda con los ojos fijos en un punto.*)

    Te diré, niño mío, que sí
    Tronchada y rota soy para ti.
    ¡Cómo me duele esta cintura
    donde tendrás primera cuna!
    ¿Cuándo, mi niño, vas a venir?
    «¡Cuando tu carne huela a jazmín!»

Telón

CUADRO SEGUNDO

Campo. Sale YERMA. *Trae una cesta.* (*Sale la* VIEJA 1.ª.)¹⁸

YERMA.   Buenos días.

VIEJA.   Buenos los tenga la hermosa muchacha.¹⁹ ¿Dónde vas?

YERMA.   Vengo de llevar la comida a mi esposo, que trabaja en los olivos.

VIEJA.   ¿Llevas mucho tiempo de casada?

YERMA.   Tres años.

VIEJA.   ¿Tienes hijos?

YERMA.   No.

VIEJA.   ¡Bah! ¡Ya tendrás!

---

¹⁷ *Tell him to dig deeper!* (See Endnote **D**).
¹⁸ This is the Vieja Pagana of the play's list of characters.
¹⁹ *And a good day to you my pretty.*

YERMA. (*Con ansia.*) ¿Usted lo cree?

VIEJA. ¿Por qué no? (*Se sienta.*) También yo vengo de traer la comida a mi esposo. Es viejo. Todavía trabaja. Tengo nueve hijos como nueve soles, pero, como ninguno es hembra, aquí me tienes a mí de un lado para otro.[20]

YERMA. Usted vive al otro lado del río.

VIEJA. Sí. En los molinos. ¿De qué familia eres tú?

YERMA. Yo soy hija de Enrique el pastor.

VIEJA. ¡Ah! Enrique el pastor. Lo conocí. Buena gente. Levantarse, sudar, comer unos panes y morirse. Ni más juego, ni más nada. Las ferias para otros.[21] Criaturas de silencio. Pude haberme casado con un tío tuyo. Pero ¡ca![22] Yo he sido una mujer de faldas en el aire, he ido flechada[23] a la tajada de melón, a la fiesta, a la torta de azúcar. Muchas veces me he asomado de madrugada a la puerta creyendo oír música de bandurrias[24] que iba, que venía, pero era el aire. (*Ríe.*) Te vas a reír de mí. He tenido dos maridos, catorce hijos, seis murieron, y sin embargo no estoy triste y quisiera vivir mucho más. Es lo que digo yo: las higueras, ¡cuánto duran!; las casas, ¡cuánto duran!; y sólo nosotras, las endemoniadas mujeres, nos hacemos polvo por cualquier cosa.[25]

YERMA. Yo quisiera hacerle una pregunta.

VIEJA. ¿A ver? (*La mira.*) Ya sé lo que me vas a decir. De estas cosas no se puede decir palabra. (*Se levanta.*)

YERMA. (*Deteniéndola.*) ¿Por qué no? Me ha dado confianza el

---

[20] *I've nine bonny children, but not one of them's a girl, so here I am, still fetching and carrying.*

[21] *Fun, not a scrap. Jaunting off to fairs wasn't for them.* Yerma's poor, upright and frivolity-shunning family background is an important part of her psychological make-up.

[22] *Not likely!*

[23] *I simply couldn't resist.*

[24] A traditional lute-like instrument. The items the Vieja 1.ª mentions here are all associated with country fairs and celebrations.

[25] *It's just us damn women that are worn down to a frazzle by the least thing.*

oírla hablar. Hace tiempo estoy deseando tener conversación con una mujer vieja. Porque yo quiero enterarme. Sí. Usted me dirá…

VIEJA. ¿Qué?

YERMA. (*Bajando la voz.*) Lo que usted sabe. ¿Por qué estoy yo seca? ¿Me he de quedar en plena vida para cuidar aves o poner cortinitas planchadas en mi ventanillo? No. Usted me ha de decir lo que tengo que hacer, que yo haré lo que sea; aunque me mande clavarme agujas en el sitio más débil de mis ojos.[26]

VIEJA. ¿Yo? Yo no sé nada. Yo me he puesto boca arriba y he comenzado a cantar.[27] Los hijos llegan como el agua. ¡Ay! ¿Quién puede decir que este cuerpo que tienes no es hermoso? Pisas, y al fondo de la calle relincha el caballo. ¡Ay! Déjame, muchacha, no me hagas hablar. Pienso muchas ideas que no quiero decir.

YERMA. ¿Por qué? Con mi marido no hablo de otra cosa.

VIEJA. Oye. ¿A ti te gusta tu marido?

YERMA. ¿Cómo?

VIEJA. ¿Que si lo quieres? ¿Si deseas estar con él?…

YERMA. No sé.

VIEJA. ¿No tiemblas cuando se acerca a ti? ¿No te da así como un sueño cuando acerca sus labios? Dime.

YERMA. No. No lo he sentido nunca.

VIEJA. ¿Nunca? ¿Ni cuando has bailado?

YERMA. (*Recordando.*) Quizá… Una vez… Víctor…

VIEJA. Sigue.

YERMA. Me cogió de la cintura y no pude decirle nada porque no podía hablar. Otra vez, el mismo Víctor, teniendo yo catorce años (él era un zagalón), me cogió en sus brazos para saltar una

[26] See Endnote E.
[27] Yerma also sang on her wedding night (see 1, 1). While Yerma's songs are invocations of a child, the Vieja's singing celebrated sexual enjoyment.

45

acequia y me entró un temblor que me sonaron los dientes. Pero es que yo he sido vergonzosa.

VIEJA.   ¿Y con tu marido?…

YERMA.   Mi marido es otra cosa. Me lo dio mi padre y yo lo acepté. Con alegría. Esta es la pura verdad. Pues el primer día que me puse novia con él ya pensé… en los hijos… Y me miraba en sus ojos. Sí, pero era para verme muy chica, muy manejable, como si yo fuera hija mía.[28]

VIEJA.   Todo lo contrario que yo. Quizá por eso no hayas parido a tiempo. Los hombres tienen que gustar, muchacha. Han de deshacernos las trenzas y darnos de beber agua en su misma boca. Así corre el mundo.

YERMA.   El tuyo, que el mío, no. Yo pienso muchas cosas, muchas, y estoy segura que las cosas que pienso las ha de realizar mi hijo. Yo me entregué a mi marido por él, y me sigo entregando para ver si llega, pero nunca por divertirme.

VIEJA.   ¡Y resulta que estás vacía!

YERMA.   No, vacía no, porque me estoy llenando de odio. Dime, ¿tengo yo la culpa? ¿Es preciso buscar en el hombre al hombre nada más? Entonces, ¿qué vas a pensar cuando te deja en la cama con los ojos tristes mirando al techo y da media vuelta y se duerme? ¿He de quedarme pensando en él o en lo que puede salir relumbrando de mi pecho? Yo no sé, pero dímelo tú por caridad. (*Se arrodilla.*)

VIEJA.   ¡Ay qué flor abierta! ¡Qué criatura tan hermosa eres! Déjame. No me hagas hablar más. No quiero hablarte más. Son asuntos de honra y yo no quemo la honra de nadie. Tú sabrás. De todos modos, debías ser menos inocente.

YERMA. (*Triste.*)   Las muchachas que se crían en el campo, como yo, tienen cerradas todas las puertas. Todo se vuelve medias

---

[28] Yerma's notion of legitimate self-identity is at two removes of vicariousness. She defines herself as an object in her husband's dominant gaze, and, even then, merely as an instrument (the bearer of his child) rather than a person in her own right.

palabras, gestos, porque todas estas cosas dicen que no se pueden saber. Y tú también, tú también te callas y te vas con aire de doctora, sabiéndolo todo, pero negándolo a la que se muere de sed.

VIEJA.   A otra mujer serena yo le hablaría. A ti, no.[29] Soy vieja y sé lo que digo.

YERMA.   Entonces, que Dios me ampare.

VIEJA.   Dios, no. A mí no me ha gustado nunca Dios. ¿Cuándo os vais a dar cuenta de que no existe? Son los hombres los que te tienen que amparar.

YERMA.   Pero ¿por qué me dices eso?, ¿por qué?

VIEJA.   (*Yéndose.*) Aunque debía haber Dios, aunque fuera pequeñito, para que mandara rayos contra los hombres de simiente podrida que encharcan la alegría de los campos.[30]

YERMA.   No sé lo que me quieres decir.

VIEJA.   (*Sigue.*)   Bueno, yo me entiendo. No pases tristeza. Espera en firme. Eres muy joven todavía. ¿Qué quieres que haga yo?[31] (*Se va.*)

(*Aparecen dos* MUCHACHAS.)

MUCHACHA 1.ª   Por todas partes nos vamos encontrando gente.

YERMA.   Con las faenas, los hombres están en los olivos, hay que traerles de comer. No quedan en las casas más que los ancianos.

MUCHACHA 2.ª   ¿Tú regresas al pueblo?

YERMA.   Hacia allá voy.

MUCHACHA 1.ª   Yo llevo mucha prisa. Me dejé al niño dormido no hay nadie en casa.

YERMA.   Pues aligera, mujer. Los niños no se pueden dejar solos. ¿Hay cerdos en tu casa?

---

[29] See Endnote **F**.

[30] See Endnote **G**.

[31] The Vieja 1.ª again hints that the remedy lies in Yerma's own hands.

MUCHACHA l.ª   No. Pero tienes razón.[32] Voy deprisa.

YERMA.   Anda. Así pasan las cosas. Seguramente lo has dejado encerrado.

MUCHACHA l.ª   Es natural.

YERMA.   Sí, pero es que no os dais cuenta lo que es un niño pequeño. La causa que nos parece más inofensiva puede acabar con él. Una agujita, un sorbo de agua.

MUCHACHA l.ª   Tienes razón. Voy corriendo. Es que no me doy bien cuenta de las cosas.

YERMA.   Anda.

MUCHACHA 2.ª   Si tuvieras cuatro o cinco, no hablarías así.

YERMA.   ¿Por qué? Aunque tuviera cuarenta.

MUCHACHA 2.ª   De todos modos, tú y yo, con no tenerlos, vivimos más tranquilas.

YERMA.   Yo, no.

MUCHACHA 2.ª   Yo, sí. ¡Qué afán![33] En cambio mi madre no hace más que darme yerbajos para que los tenga y en octubre iremos al Santo que dicen que los da a la que lo pide con ansia. Mi madre pedirá. Yo, no.

YERMA.   ¿Por qué te has casado?

MUCHACHA 2.ª   Porque me han casado. Se casan todas. Si seguimos así, no va a haber solteras más que las niñas. Bueno y además…, una se casa en realidad mucho antes de ir a la iglesia. Pero las viejas se empeñan en todas esta cosas. Yo tengo diecinueve años y no me gusta guisar, ni lavar. Bueno, pues todo el día he de estar haciendo, lo que no me gusta. ¿Y para qué? ¿Qué necesidad tiene mi marido de ser mi marido? Porque lo mismo, hacíamos de novios que ahora. Tonterías de los viejos.

YERMA.   Calla, no digas esas cosas.

MUCHACHA 2.ª   También tú me dirás loca. «¡La loca, la loca!»

---

[32] i.e the pigs might attack the unattended infant (see Endnote **H**).
[33] *It's not worth the bother.*

(*Ríe.*) Yo te puedo decir lo único que he aprendido en la vida: toda la gente está metida dentro de sus casas haciendo lo que no les gusta. Cuánto mejor se está en medio de la calle. Ya voy al arroyo, ya subo a tocar las campanas, ya me tomo un refresco de anís.

YERMA. Eres una niña.

MUCHACHA 2.ª Claro, pero no estoy loca. (*Ríe.*)

YERMA. ¿Tu madre vive en la parte más alta del pueblo?

MUCHACHA 2.ª Sí.

YERMA. ¿En la última casa?

MUCHACHA 2.ª Sí.

YERMA. ¿Cómo se llama?

MUCHACHA 2.ª Dolores. ¿Por qué preguntas?

YERMA. Por nada.

MUCHACHA 2.ª Por algo preguntarás.

YERMA. No sé…, es un decir…[34]

MUCHACHA 2.ª Allá tú… Mira, me voy a dar la comida a mi marido. (*Ríe.*) Es lo que hay que ver.[35] ¡Qué lástima no poder decir mi novio! ¿Verdad? ¡Ya se va la loca! (*Se va riendo alegremente.*) ¡Adiós![36]

VOZ DE VÍCTOR. (*Cantando.*)

¿Por qué duermes solo, pastor?
¿Por qué duermes solo, pastor?
En mi colcha de lana
dormirías mejor.
¿Por qué duermes solo, pastor?

YERMA. (*Escuchando.*)

¿Por qué duermes solo, pastor?

[34] *I was only wondering.* Yerma is already considering the idea of consulting Dolores.
[35] *It just goes to show!*
[36] See Endnote I.

En mi colcha de lana
dormirías mejor.
Tu colcha de oscura piedra,
   pastor,
y tu camisa de escarcha,
   pastor,
juncos grises del invierno
en la noche de tu cama.
Los robles ponen agujas,
   pastor,
debajo de tu almohada,
   pastor,
y si oyes voz de mujer
es la rota voz del agua.
   Pastor, pastor.
¿Qué quiere el monte de ti,
   pastor?
Monte de hierbas amargas,
¿qué niño te está matando?
¡La espina de la retama!

(Va a salir y se tropieza con VÍCTOR, *que entra.)*

VÍCTOR. (*Alegre.*)   ¿Dónde va lo hermoso?

YERMA.   ¿Cantabas tú?

VÍCTOR.   Yo.

YERMA.   ¡Qué bien! Nunca te había sentido.[37]

VÍCTOR.   ¿No?

YERMA.   Y qué voz tan pujante. Parece un chorro de agua[38] que te llena toda la boca.

VÍCTOR.   Soy alegre.

YERMA.   Es verdad.

---

[37] I've never heard you sing before.
[38] like a gush of water; in parts of southern Andalusia a mountain waterfall is termed 'chorro'.

VÍCTOR.   Como tú triste.

YERMA.   No soy triste. Es que tengo motivos para estarlo.

VÍCTOR.   Y tu marido más triste que tú.

YERMA.   Él sí. Tiene un carácter seco.

VÍCTOR.   Siempre fue igual. (*Pausa.* YERMA *está sentada.*) ¿Viniste a traer la comida?

YERMA.   Sí. (*Lo mira. Pausa.*) ¿Qué tienes aquí? (*Senala la cara.*)

VÍCTOR.   ¿Dónde?

YERMA. (*Se levanta y se acerca a* VÍCTOR.)   Aquí..., en la mejilla, como una quemadura.

VÍCTOR.   No es nada.

YERMA.   Me había parecido.

(*Pausa.*)

VÍCTOR.   Debe ser el sol...

YERMA.   Quizá... (*Pausa. El silencio se acentúa y sin el menor gesto comienza una lucha[39] entre los dos personajes.*) (*Temblando.*) ¿Oyes?

VÍCTOR.   ¿Qué?

YERMA.   ¿No sientes llorar?

VÍCTOR. (*Escuchando.*)   No.

YERMA.   Me había parecido que lloraba un niño.[40]

VÍCTOR.   ¿Sí?

YERMA.   Muy cerca. Y lloraba como ahogado.

---

[39] Yerma seems to be unconsciously challenging Víctor to make a move; her show of concern for a sunburn on his cheek might seem deliberately flirtatious in a less earnest person.

[40] Lorca gave this perception as an example of 'psychological' effects in his characterization of Yerma. Her subconscious memories of adolescent feelings for Victor come to the surface, inextricably confused with her longing for a child (*Conv.* 42). (See fn. [12], p. 4.)

VÍCTOR.   Por aquí hay siempre muchos niños que vienen a robar fruta.

YERMA.   No. Es la voz de un niño pequeño.

(*Pausa.*)

VÍCTOR.   No oigo nada.

YERMA.   Serán ilusiones mías. (*Lo mira fijamente, y* VÍCTOR *la mira también y desvía la mirada lentamente, como con miedo.*[41])

(*Sale* JUAN.)

JUAN.   ¿Qué haces todavía aquí?

YERMA.   Hablaba.

VÍCTOR.   Salud. (*Sale.*)

JUAN.   Debías estar en casa.

YERMA.   Me entretuve.

JUAN.   No comprendo en qué te has entretenido.[42]

YERMA.   Oí cantar los pájaros.

JUAN.   Está bien. Así darás que hablar a las gentes.

YERMA. (*Fuerte.*)   Juan, ¿qué piensas?

JUAN.   No lo digo por ti, lo digo por las gentes.

YERMA.   ¡Puñalada que le den a las gentes![43]

JUAN.   No maldigas. Está feo en una mujer.

YERMA.   Ojalá fuera yo una mujer.[44]

JUAN.   Vamos a dejarnos de conversación. Vete a la casa.

(*Pausa.*)

---

[41] See Endnote **J**.

[42] Juan suspiciously exploits a double meaning, 'to be delayed' and 'to loiter, amuse onseself'.

[43] *Other people! I hope they choke!* (lit. 'get stabbed').

[44] *If only I were a woman.* Yerma's challenges to restrictive moral definitions have moved beyond questioning the rules governing social conduct to casting herself as an existential outcast.

YERMA.   Está bien. ¿Te espero?

JUAN.   No. Estaré toda la noche regando. Viene poca agua, es mía hasta la salida del sol y tengo que defenderla de los ladrones.[45] Te acuestas y te duermes.

YERMA. (*Dramática*.)   ¡Me dormiré![46] (*Sale*.)

Telón

---

[45] See Endnote **K**.
[46] Yerma's ironic echoing exploits the symbolic meaning of sleep as a subduing of vital energies, a retreat from living.

Acto Segundo

CUADRO PRIMERO

Torrente donde lavan las mujeres del pueblo. Las LAVANDERAS *están situadas en varios planos. Cantan.*[47]

(*Canto a telón corrido.*)

> En el arroyo frío
> lavo tu cinta.
> Como un jazmín caliente
> tienes la risa.

LAVANDERA 1.ª   A mí no me gusta hablar.

LAVANDERA 3.ª   Pero aquí se habla.

LAVANDERA 4.ª   Y no hay mal en ello.

LAVANDERA 5.ª   La que quiera honra, que la gane.[48]

LAVANDERA 4.ª

> Yo planté un tomillo,
> yo lo vi crecer.
> El que quiera honra,
> que se porte bien.

(*Ríen.*)

LAVANDERA 5.ª   Así se habla.

LAVANDERA 1.ª   Pero es que nunca se sabe nada.

LAVANDERA 4.ª   Lo cierto es que el marido se ha llevado a vivir con ellos a sus dos hermanas.

LAVANDERA 5.ª   ¿Las solteras?

---

[47] See Endnote **L**.

[48] *Honour is as honour does* (lit. 'if a woman who wants a good name she should earn it'). Yerma is never openly identified in the scene (the only one in which she does not appear), but the play's audience will naturally assume it is the main character who is the object of comment.

LAVANDERA 4.ª   Sí. Estaban encargadas de cuidar la iglesia y ahora cuidan de su cuñada. Yo no podría vivir con ellas.

LAVANDERA 1.ª   ¿Por qué?

LAVANDERA 4.ª   Porque dan miedo. Son como esas hojas grandes que nacen de pronto sobre los sepulcros. Están untadas con cera. Son metidas hacia adentro. Se me figura que guisan su comida con el aceite de las lámparas.[49]

LAVANDERA 3.ª   ¿Y están ya en la casa?

LAVANDERA 4.ª   Desde ayer. El marido sale otra vez a sus tierras.

LAVANDERA 1.ª   ¿,Pero se puede saber lo que ha ocurrido?

LAVANDERA 5.ª   Anteanoche, ella la pasó sentada en el tranco, a pesar del frío.

LAVANDERA 1.ª   Pero, ¿por qué?

LAVANDERA 4.ª   Le cuesta trabajo estar en su casa.[50]

LAVANDERA 5.ª   Estas machorras[51] son así: cuando podían estar haciendo encajes o confituras de manzanas, les gusta subirse al tejado y andar descalzas por esos ríos.

LAVANDERA 1.ª   ¿Quién eres tú para decir estas cosas? Ella no tiene hijos, pero no es por culpa suya.

LAVANDERA 4.ª   Tiene hijos la que quiere tenerlos. Es que las regalonas, las flojas, las endulzadas, no son a propósito para llevar el vientre arrugado.[52]

(*Ríen.*)

LAVANDERA 3.ª   Y se echan polvos de blancura y colorete y se prenden ramos de adelfa en busca de otro que no es su marido.

---

[49] The sisters, it is claimed, have a pallid, waxy complexion from spending so much time in church, and are so obsessed with notions of piety and respectability that they cook with oil from church lamps.

[50] *She can't stand being indoors.*

[51] See Endnote **M**.

[52] *These pampered, feeble softies are no good for getting stretch marks on their bellies.* There is malicious envy here for Yerma's comfortable life as the wife of a successful farmer.

LAVANDERA 5.ª   ¡No hay otra verdad![53]

LAVANDERA 1.ª   Pero ¿vosotras la habéis visto con otro?

LAVANDERA 4.ª   Nosotras no, pero las gentes sí.

LAVANDERA 1.ª   ¡Siempre las gentes!

LAVANDERA 5.ª   Dicen que en dos ocasiones.

LAVANDERA 2.ª   ¿Y qué hacían?

LAVANDERA 4.ª   Hablaban.

LAVANDERA 1.ª   Hablar no es pecado.

LAVANDERA 5.ª   Hay una cosa en el mundo que es la mirada. Mi madre lo decía. No es lo mismo una mujer mirando a unas rosas que una mujer mirando a los muslos de un hombre. Ella lo mira.

LAVANDERA 1.ª   ¿Pero a quién?

LAVANDERA 4.ª   A uno. ¿Lo oyes? Entérate tú.[54] ¿Quieres que lo diga más alto? (*Risas.*) Y cuando no lo mira, porque está sola, porque no lo tiene delante, lo lleva retratado en los ojos.[55]

LAVANDERA 1.ª   ¡Eso es mentira!

(*Algazara.*)

LAVANDERA 5.ª   ¿Y el marido?

LAVANDERA 3.ª   El marido está como sordo. Parado como un lagarto puesto al sol.[56]

(*Ríen.*)

LAVANDERA 1.ª   Todo esto se arreglaría si tuvieran criaturas.

LAVANDERA 2.ª   Todo esto son cuestiones de gente que no tiene conformidad con su sino.

LAVANDERA 4.ª   Cada hora que transcurre aumenta el infierno en

---

[53] *And that's the absolute truth.*

[54] *A certain someone, got it? Use your loaf!*

[55] See Endnote N.

[56] *Her husband turns a deaf ear. He just does nothing, like a lizard sunning itself.* Juan, too, is to admit that he is not 'firm' enough with his wife. Here he attracts the traditional scorn for complaisant husbands.

aquella casa. Ella y las cuñadas, sin despegar los labios, blanquean todo el día las paredes, friegan los cobres, limpian con vaho los cristales, dan aceite a la solería. Pues, cuando más relumbra la vivienda, más arde por dentro.[57]

LAVANDERA 1.ª   Él tiene la culpa, él. Cuando un padre no da hijos debe cuidar de su mujer.

LAVANDERA 4.ª   La culpa es de ella, que tiene por lengua un pedernal.

LAVANDERA 1.ª   ¿Qué demonio se te ha metido entre los cabellos para que hables así?

LAVANDERA 4.ª   ¿Y quién ha dado licencia a tu boca para que me des consejos?[58]

LAVANDERA 5.ª   ¡Callar!

(*Risas.*)

LAVANDERA 1.ª   Con una aguja de hacer calceta ensartaría yo las lenguas murmuradoras.

LAVANDERA 5.ª   ¡Calla!

LAVANDERA 4.ª   Y yo la tapa del pecho de las fingidas.[59]

LAVANDERA 5.ª   Silencio. ¿No ves que por ahí vienen las cuñadas?

(*Murmullos. Entran las dos* CUÑADAS *de* YERMA. *Van vestidas de luto. Se ponen a lavar en medio de un silencio. Se oyen esquilas.*)

LAVANDERA 1.ª   ¿Se van ya los zagales?

LAVANDERA 3.ª   Sí, ahora salen todos los rebaños.

LAVANDERA 4.ª (*Aspirando.*)   Me gusta el olor de las ovejas.

LAVANDERA 3.ª   ¿Sí?

[57] *The more spotless a house on the outside, the hotter the flames on the inside.* This comment both alludes to notions of hypocrisy and expresses a psychological perception that over-zealous domestic cleaning betrays the repression of violent emotional tensions.

[58] *When I want your advice I'll ask for it!*

[59] She would likewise skewer the breast of deceitful women, the cover ('tapa') concealing their true feelings and motives.

57

LAVANDERA 4.ª   ¿Y por qué no? Olor de lo que una tiene.[60] Cómo me gusta el olor del fango rojo que trae el río por el invierno.

LAVANDERA 3.ª   Caprichos.

LAVANDERA 5.ª (*Mirando.*)   Van juntos todos los rebaños.

LAVANDERA 4.ª   Es una inundación de lana. Arramblan con todo. Si los trigos verdes tuvieran cabeza, temblarían de verlos venir.

LAVANDERA 3.ª   ¡Mira como corren! ¡Qué manada de enemigos![61]

LAVANDERA 1.ª   Ya salieron todos, no falta uno.

LAVANDERA 4.ª   A ver… No… sí, sí falta uno.

LAVANDERA 5.ª   ¿Cuál?…

LAVANDERA 4.ª   El de Víctor.

(*Las dos* CUÑADAS *se yerguen y miran.*)

> En el arroyo frío
> lavo tu cinta.
> Como un jazmín caliente
> tienes la risa.
> Quiero vivir
> en la nevada chica
> de ese jazmín.

LAVANDERA 1.ª
> ¡Ay de la casada seca![62]
> ¡Ay de la que tiene los pechos de arena!

LAVANDERA 5.ª
> Dime si tu marido
> guarda semilla
> para que el agua cante
> por tu camisa.

LAVANDERA 4.ª
> Es tu camisa

---

[60] *good, familiar smells* (lit. 'the smell of what one has').
[61] *What a mighty host!*
[62] *Pity the barren wife!*.

nave de plata y viento
por las orillas.

LAVANDERA 3.ª

Las ropas de mi niño
vengo a lavar,
para que tome al agua
lecciones de cristal.[63]

LAVANDERA 2.ª

Por el monte ya llega
mi marido a comer.
Él me trae una rosa
y yo le doy tres.[64]

LAVANDERA 5.ª

Por el llano ya vino
mi marido a cenar.
Las brasas que me entrega
cubro con arrayán.

LAVANDERA 4.ª

Por el aire ya viene
mi marido a dormir.
Yo alhelíes rojos
y él rojo alhelí.

LAVANDERA 3.ª

Hay que juntar flor con flor
cuando el verano seca la sangre al segador.

LAVANDERA 4.ª

Y abrir el vientre a pájaros sin sueño
cuando a la puerta llama tembloroso el invierno.

LAVANDERA 1.ª

Hay que gemir en la sábana.

---

[63] i.e., so the shining whiteness of the washed baby-clothes will outdo the water (give it a lesson) in clarity and purity.

[64] This, and the following verses, frankly celebrate the joy of sex – but invariably in a socially legitimate context of a husband returning from outdoor work to a wife at home.

LAVANDERA 4.ª

   ¡Y hay que cantar!

LAVANDERA 5.ª

   Cuando el hombre nos trae
   la corona y el pan.

LAVANDERA 4.ª

   Porque los brazos se enlazan.

LAVANDERA 5.ª

   Porque la luz se nos quiebra en la garganta.

LAVANDERA 4.ª

   Porque se endulza el tallo de las ramas.

LAVANDERA 5.ª

   Y las tiendas del viento cubran a las montañas.

LAVANDERA 6.ª (*Apareciendo en lo alto del torrente.*)

   Para que un niño funda
   yertos vidrios del alba.[65]

LAVANDERA 4.ª

   Y nuestro cuerpo tiene
   ramas furiosas de coral.

LAVANDERA 5.ª

   Para que haya remeros
   en las aguas del mar.

LAVANDERA 1.ª

   Un niño pequeño, un niño.

LAVANDERA 2.ª

   Y las palomas abren las alas y el pico.

LAVANDERA 3.ª

   Un niño que gime, un hijo.

LAVANDERA 4.ª

   Y los hombres avanzan
   como ciervos heridos.

---

[65] A sixth laundress appears, to sum up the central significance of childbirth: the bringing of light, warmth and life into a cold, bleak world.

LAVANDERA 5.ª

¡Alegría, alegría, alegría
del vientre redondo bajo la camisa!

LAVANDERA 2.ª

¡Alegría, alegría, alegría,
ombligo, cáliz tierno de maravilla!

LAVANDERA 1.ª

¡Pero ay de la casada seca!
¡Ay de la que tiene los pechos de arena!

LAVANDERA 4.ª

¡Que relumbre!

LAVANDERA 5.ª

¡Que corra!

LAVANDERA 4.ª

¡Que vuelva a relumbrar!

LAVANDERA 3.ª

¡Que cante!

LAVANDERA 2.ª

¡Que se esconda!

LAVANDERA 3.ª

Y que vuelva a cantar.

LAVANDERA 6.ª

La aurora que mi niño
lleva en el delantal

LAVANDERA 4.ª (*Cantan todas a coro.*)

En el arroyo frío
lavo tu cinta.
Como un jazmín caliente
tienes la risa.
¡Ja, ja, ja!

(*Mueven los paños con ritmo y los golpean.*)

Telón

CUADRO SEGUNDO

Casa de YERMA. *Atardecer.* JUAN *está sentado. Las dos* HERMANAS *de pie.*

JUAN.   ¿Dices que salió hace poco? (*La* HERMANA *mayor contesta con la cabeza.*) Debe estar en la fuente. Pero ya sabéis que no me gusta que salga sola. (*Pausa.*) Puedes poner la mesa. (*Sale la* HERMANA *menor.*) Bien ganado tengo el pan que como. (*A su* HERMANA.) Ayer pasé un día duro. Estuve podando los manzanos y a la caída de la tarde me puse a pensar para qué pondría yo tanta ilusión en la faena si no puedo llevarme una manzana a la boca. Estoy harto. (*Se pasa las manos por la cara. Pausa.*) Ésa no viene[66]... Una de vosotras debía salir con ella, porque para eso estáis aquí comiendo en mi mantel y bebiendo mi vino. Mi vida está en el campo, pero mi honra está aquí. Y mi honra es también la vuestra. (*La* HERMANA *inclina la cabeza.*) No lo tomes a mal.[67] (*Entra* YERMA *con dos cántaros. Queda parada en la puerta.*) ¡Vienes de la fuente?

YERMA.   Para tener agua fresca en la comida. (*Sale la otra* HERMANA.) ¿Cómo están las tierras?

JUAN.   Ayer estuve podando los árboles.

(YERMA *deja los cántaros. Pausa.*)

YERMA.   Te quedarás?

JUAN.   He de cuidar el ganado. Tú sabes que esto es cosa del dueño.

YERMA.   Lo sé muy bien. No lo repitas.

JUAN.   Cada hombre tiene su vida.

YERMA.   Y cada mujer la suya. No te pido yo que te quedes. Aquí tengo todo lo que necesito. Tus hermanas me guardan bien. Pan tierno y requesón y cordero asado como yo aquí, y pasto lleno de

---

[66] *She's still not back.* Juan's feeling of estrangement from his wife is evident in the demonstrative, 'that woman'.

[67] *Don't take it the wrong way.* (See Endnote **O**).

rocío tus ganados en el monte.[68] Creo que puedes vivir en paz.

JUAN.   Para vivir en paz se necesita estar tranquilo.

YERMA.   ¿Y tú no estás?

JUAN.   No estoy.

YERMA.   Desvía la intención.[69]

JUAN.   ¿Es que no conoces mi modo de ser? Las ovejas en el redil y las mujeres en su casa. Tú sales demasiado. ¿No me has oído decir esto siempre?

YERMA.   Justo. Las mujeres dentro de sus casas. Cuando las casas no son tumbas. Cuando las sillas se rompen y las sábanas de hilo se gastan con el uso. Pero aquí, no. Cada noche, cuando me acuesto, encuentro mi cama más nueva, más reluciente, como si estuviera recién traída de la ciudad.

JUAN.   Tú misma reconoces que llevo razón al quejarme. ¡Que tengo motivos para estar alerta!

YERMA.   Alerta ¿de qué? En nada te ofendo. Vivo sumisa a ti, y lo que sufro lo guardo pegado a mis carnes.[70] Y cada día que pase será peor. Vamos a callarnos. Yo sabré llevar mi cruz como mejor pueda, pero no me preguntes nada. Si pudiera de pronto volverme vieja y tuviera la boca como una flor machacada, te podría sonreír y conllevar la vida contigo. Ahora, ahora, déjame con mis clavos.[71]

JUAN.   Hablas de una manera que yo no te entiendo. No te privo de nada. Mando a los pueblos vecinos por las cosas que te gustan. Yo tengo mis defectos, pero quiero tener paz y sosiego contigo. Quiero dormir fuera y pensar que tú duermes también.

YERMA.   Pero yo no duermo, yo no puedo dormir.

[68] Yerma accuses him of regarding her as a material investment to be well looked after, like his sheep.

[69] *Don't bring that up.*

[70] *I keep it well inside me.* (lit. 'stuck to my flesh') One of Yerma's characteristically physical expressions of her feelings.

[71] Yerma vividly extends the commonplace expression 'a cross to bear' by likening her suffering to being nailed to one.

JUAN.   ¿Es que te falta algo? Dime. (*Pausa.*) ¡Contesta!

YERMA. (*Con intención y mirando fijamente al marido.*)   Sí, me falta. (*Pausa.*)

JUAN.   Siempre lo mismo. Hace ya más de cinco años. Yo casi lo estoy olvidando.

YERMA.   Pero yo no soy tú. Los hombres tienen otra vida: los ganados, los árboles, las conversaciones; y las mujeres no tenemos más que esta de la cría y el cuido de la cría.

JUAN.   Todo el mundo no es igual. ¿Por qué no te traes un hijo de tu hermano? Yo no me opongo.

YERMA.   No quiero cuidar hijos de otras. Me figuro que se me van a helar los brazos de tenerlos.

JUAN.   Con este achaque vives alocada, sin pensar en lo que debías, y te empeñas en meter la cabeza por una roca.

YERMA.   Roca que es una infamia que sea roca, porque debía ser un canasto de flores y agua dulce.

JUAN.   Estando a tu lado no se siente más que inquietud, desasosiego. En último caso debes resignarte.

YERMA.   Yo he venido a estas cuatro paredes para no resignarme. Cuando tenga la cabeza atada con un pañuelo para que no se me abra la boca, y las manos bien amarradas dentro del ataúd, en esa hora me habré resignado.[72]

JUAN.   Entonces, ¿qué quieres hacer?

YERMA.   Quiero beber agua y no hay vaso ni agua; quiero subir al monte y no tengo pies; quiero bordar mis enaguas y no encuentro los hilos.

JUAN.   Lo que pasa es que no eres una mujer verdadera y buscas la ruina de un hombre sin voluntad.

YERMA.   Yo no sé quién soy. Déjame andar y desahogarme. En nada te he faltado.

---

[72] See Endnote **P**.

JUAN.   No me gusta que la gente me señale. Por eso quiero ver cerrada esa puerta y cada persona en su casa.

(*Sale la* HERMANA 1.ª *lentamente y se acerca a una alacena.*)

YERMA.   Hablar con la gente no es pecado.

JUAN.   Pero puede parecerlo. (*Sale la otra* HERMANA *y se dirige a los cántaros, en los cuales llena una jarra.*) (*Bajando la voz.*) Yo no tengo fuerzas para esta cosas. Cuando te den conversación, cierra la boca y piensa que eres una mujer casada.

YERMA. (*Con asombro.*)   ¡Casada!

JUAN.   Y que las familias tienen honra y la honra es una carga que se lleva entre todos.[73] (*Sale la* HERMANA *con la jarra, lentamente.*) Pero que está oscura y débil en los mismos caños de la sangre.[74] (*Sale la otra* HERMANA *con una fuente, de modo casi procesional. Pausa.*) Perdóname. (YERMA *mira a su marido; éste levanta la cabeza y se tropieza con la mirada.*) Aunque me miras de un modo que no debía decirte perdóname, sino obligarte, encerrarte, porque para eso soy el marido.

(*Aparecen las dos* HERMANAS *en la puerta.*)

YERMA.   Te ruego que no hables. Deja quieta la cuestión.

(*Pausa.*)

JUAN.   Vamos a comer. (*Entran las* HERMANAS. *Pausa.*) ¿Me has oído?

YERMA. (*Dulce.*)   Come tú con tus hermanas. Yo no tengo hambre todavía.

JUAN.   Lo que quieras. (*Entra.*)

YERMA. (*Como soñando.*)
     ¡Ay qué prado de pena!
     ¡Ay qué puerta cerrada a la herrnosura,
     que pido un hijo que sufrir y el aire
     me ofrece dalias de dormida luna!

[73] *The upkeep of honour involves the whole family.*
[74] *in the very blood of our veins.*

Estos dos manantiales que yo tengo
de leche tibia, son en la espesura
de mi carne, dos pulsos de caballo,
que hacen latir la rama de mi angustia.
¡Ay pechos ciegos bajo mi vestido!
¡Ay palomas sin ojos ni blancura!
¡Ay qué dolor de sangre prisionera
me está clavando avispas en la nuca!
Pero tú has de venir, ¡amor!, mi niño,
porque el agua da sal, la tierra fruta,
y nuestro vientre guarda tiernos hijos
como la nube lleva dulce lluvia.

(*Mlra hacia la puerta.*)

¡María! ¿Por qué pasas tan deprisa por mi puerta?

MARÍA. (*Entra con un niño en brazos.*)　　Cuando voy con el niño, lo hago… ¡Como siempre lloras!…

YERMA.　　Tienes razón. (*Coge al niño y se sienta.*)

MARÍA.　　Me da tristeza que tengas envidia.

YERMA.　　No es envidia lo que tengo; es pobreza.

MARÍA.　　No te quejes.

YERMA.　　¡Cómo no me voy a quejar cuando te veo a ti y a las otras mujeres llenas por dentro de flores, y viéndome yo inútil en medio de tanta hermosura!

MARÍA.　　Pero tienes otras cosas. Si me oyeras, podrías ser feliz.

YERMA.　　La mujer del campo que no da hijos es inútil como un manojo de espinos ¡y hasta mala!, a pesar de que yo sea de este desecho dejado de la mano de Dios.[75] (MARÍA *hace un gesto como para tomar al niño.*) Tómalo; contigo está más a gusto. Yo no debo tener manos de madre.

MARÍA.　　¿Por qué me dices eso?

YERMA. (*Se levanta.*)　　Porque estoy harta, porque estoy harta de

---

[75] *(I say it) even though I belong to this God-forsaken waste.*

tenerlas y no poderlas usar en cosa propia. Que estoy ofendida, ofendida y rebajada hasta lo último, viendo que los trigos apuntan, que las fuentes no cesan de dar agua, y que paren las ovejas cientos de corderos, y las perras, y que parece que todo el campo puesto de pie me enseña sus crías tiernas, adormiladas, mientras yo siento dos golpes de martillo aquí, en lugar de la boca de mi niño.

MARÍA.   No me gusta lo que dices.

YERMA.   Las mujeres, cuando tenéis hijos, no podéis pensar en las que no los tenemos. Os quedáis frescas, ignorantes, como el que nada en agua dulce y no tiene idea de la sed.

MARÍA.   No te quiero decir lo que te digo siempre.

YERMA.   Cada vez tengo más deseos y menos esperanzas.

MARÍA.   Mala cosa.

YERMA.   Acabaré creyendo que yo misma soy mi hijo. Muchas noches bajo yo a echar la comida a los bueyes, que antes no lo hacía, porque ninguna mujer lo hace, y cuando paso por lo oscuro del cobertizo mis pasos me suenan a pasos de hombre.

MARÍA.   Cada criatura tiene su razón.

YERMA.   A pesar de todo, sigue queriéndome. ¡Ya ves cómo vivo!

MARÍA.   ¿Y tus cuñadas?

YERMA.   Muerta me vea y sin mortaja, si alguna vez les dirijo la conversación.[76]

MARÍA.   ¿Y tu marido?

YERMA.   Son tres contra mí.

MARÍA.   ¿Qué piensan?

YERMA.   Figuraciones. De gente que no tiene la conciencia tranquila. Creen que me puede gustar otro hombre y no saben

---

[76] *May I be struck down dead if I ever say a word to them.* Yerma, deeply resenting the humiliation of having the sisters set to watch over her in her own house, has vowed never to speak to them.

que, aunque me gustara, lo primero de mi casta es la honradez.[77] Son piedras delante de mí. Pero ellos no saben que yo, si quiero, puedo ser agua de arroyo que las lleve.

(*Una* HERMANA *entra y sale llevando un pan.*)

MARÍA.   De todas maneras, creo que tu marido te sigue queriendo.

YERMA.   Mi marido me da pan y casa.

MARÍA.   ¡Qué trabajos estás pasando, qué trabajos, pero acuérdate de las llagas de Nuestro Señor! (*Están en la puerta.*)

YERMA. (*Mirando al niño.*)   Ya ha despertado.

MARÍA.   Dentro de poco empezará a cantar.

YERMA.   Los mismos ojos que tú, ¿lo sabías? ¿Los has visto (*Llorando.*) ¡Tiene los mismos ojos que tú! (YERMA *empuja suavemente a* MARÍA *y ésta sale silenciosa.* YERMA *se dirige a la puerta por donde entró su marido.*)

MUCHACHA 2.ª   ¡Chisss!

YERMA. (*Volviéndose.*)   ¿Qué?

MUCHACHA 2.ª   Esperé a que saliera. Mi madre te está aguardando.

YERMA.   ¿Está sola?

MUCHACHA 2.ª   Con dos vecinas.

YERMA.   Dile que esperen un poco.

MUCHACHA 2.ª   ¿Pero vas a ir? ¿No te da miedo?

YERMA.   Voy a ir.

MUCHACHA 2.ª   ¡Allá tú![78]

YERMA.   ¡Que me esperen aunque sea tarde!

(*Entra* VÍCTOR.)

[77] *The stock I come from has always put honour and decency above everything.* Yerma's strong sense of clan and pride in carrying on its traditional virtues are central to her self-esteem.

[78] *Rather you than me.* The Second Girl, for all her blithe unconcern for traditional beliefs, is fearful of the nature and locale of the rite her mother is to perform.

VÍCTOR.   ¿Está Juan?

YERMA.   Sí

MUCHACHA 2.ª (*Cómplice.*)   Entonces yo traeré la blusa.

YERMA.   Cuando quieras. (*Sale la* MUCHACHA.) Siéntate.

VÍCTOR.   Estoy bien así.

YERMA. (*Llamando al marido.*)   ¡Juan!

VÍCTOR.   Vengo a despedirme.

YERMA.   (*Se estremece ligeramente, pero vuelve a su serenidad.*)   ¿Te vas con tus hermanos?

VÍCTOR.   Así lo quiere mi padre.

YERMA.   Ya debe estar viejo.

VÍCTOR.   Sí, muy viejo.

(*Pausa.*)

YERMA.   Haces bien en cambiar de campos.

VÍCTOR.   Todos los campos son iguales.

YERMA.   No. Yo me iría muy lejos.

VÍCTOR.   Es todo lo mismo. Las mismas ovejas tienen la misma lana.

YERMA.   Para los hombres, sí, pero las mujeres somos otra cosa. Nunca oí decir a un hombre comiendo: «¡Qué buenas son estas manzanas!» Vais a lo vuestro sin reparar en las delicadezas. De mí sé decir que he aborrecido el agua de estos pozos.

VÍCTOR.   Puede ser.

(*La escena está en una suave penumbra. Pausa.*)

YERMA.   Víctor.

VÍCTOR.   Dime.

YERMA.   ¿Por qué te vas? Aquí las gentes te quieren.

VÍCTOR.   Yo me porté bien.

(*Pausa.*)

YERMA. Te portaste bien. Siendo zagalón me llevaste una vez en brazos; ¿no recuerdas? Nunca se sabe lo que va a pasar.

VÍCTOR. Todo cambia.

YERMA. Algunas cosas no cambian. Hay cosas encerradas detrás de los muros que no pueden cambiar porque nadie las oye.

VÍCTOR. Así es.

(*Aparece la* HERMANA 2.ª *y se dirige lentamente hacia la puerta, donde queda fija iluminada por la última luz de la tarde.*)

YERMA. Pero que si salieran de pronto y gritaran, llenarían el mundo.

VÍCTOR. No se adelantaría nada. La acequia por su sitio, el rebaño en el redil, la luna en el cielo y el hombre con su arado.

YERMA. ¡Qué pena más grande no poder sentir las enseñanzas de los viejos![79]

(*Se oye el sonido largo y melancólico de las caracolas de los pastores.*)

VÍCTOR. Los rebaños.

JUAN. (*Sale.*) ¿Vas ya de camino?

VÍCTOR. Quiero pasar el puerto antes del amanecer.

JUAN. ¿Llevas alguna queja de mí?

VÍCTOR. No. Fuiste buen pagador.

JUAN. (*a* YERMA) Le compré los rebaños.

YERMA. ¿Sí?

VÍCTOR. (*a* YERMA) Tuyos son.

YERMA. No lo sabía.

JUAN. (*Satisfecho.*) Así es.

---

[79] Yerma is probably being sarcastic here. Víctor has firmly rejected her hint of breaking the barriers, and she identifies his fatalistic conformity to the established order of things and acceptance of whatever life brings as a wisdom suitable to passionless old age.

VÍCTOR.   Tu marido ha de ver su hacienda colmada.[80]

YERMA.   El fruto viene a las manos del trabajador que lo busca.

(*La* HERMANA *que está en la puerta entra dentro.*)

JUAN.   Ya no tenemos sitio donde meter tantas ovejas.

YERMA. (*Sombría.*)   La tierra es grande.

(*Pausa*)

JUAN.   Iremos juntos hasta el arroyo.

VÍCTOR.   Deseo la mayor felicidad para esta casa. (*Le da la mano a* YERMA.)

YERMA.   ¡Dios te oiga! ¡Salud!

(VÍCTOR *le da salida y, a un movimiento imperceptible de* YERMA, *se vuelve.*)

VÍCTOR.   ¿Decías algo?

YERMA. (*Dramática.*)   Salud dije.

VÍCTOR.   Gracias.

(*Salen.* YERMA *queda angustiada mirándose la mano que ha dado a* VÍCTOR. YERMA *se dirige rápidamente hacia la izquierda y toma un mantón.*)

MUCHACHA 2.ª (*En silencio, tapándole la cabeza.*)   Vamos.

YERMA.   Vamos.

(*Salen sigilosamente. La escena está casi a oscuras. Sale la* HERMANA 1.ª *con un velón que no debe dar al teatro luz ninguna, sino la natural que lleva. Se dirige al fin de la escena buscando a* YERMA. *Suenan las caracolas de los rebaños.*)

CUÑADA 1.ª (*En voz baja.*)   ¡Yerma!

(*Sale la* HERMANA 2.ª, *se miran las dos y se dirigen hacia la puerta.*)

CUÑADA 2.ª (*Más alto.*)   ¡Yerma! (*Sale.*)

---

[80] *Your husband's lands will be filled with abundance.*

CUÑADA 1.ª (*Dirigiéndose a la puerta también y con una carrasposa voz.*) ¡Yerma![81]

(*Sale. Se oyen las caracolas y los cuernos de los pastores. La escena está oscurísima.*)

Telón

---

[81] See Endnote **Q**.

Acto Tercero

CUADRO PRIMERO

Casa de la DOLORES, *la conjuradora.*[82] *Está amaneciendo. Entra* YERMA *con* DOLORES *y dos* VIEJAS.

DOLORES.   Has estado valiente.

VIEJA 1.ª[83]   No hay en el mundo fuerza como la del deseo.

VIEJA 2.ª   Pero el cementerio estaba demasiado oscuro.

DOLORES.   Muchas veces yo he hecho estas oraciones en el cementerio con mujeres que ansiaban críos, y todas han pasado miedo. Todas, menos tú.

YERMA.   Yo he venido por el resultado.[84] Creo que no eres mujer engañadora.

DOLORES.   No soy. Que mi lengua se llene de hormigas, como está la boca de los muertos, si alguna vez he mentido. La última vez hice la oración con una mujer mendicante, que estaba seca más tiempo que tú, y se le endulzó el vientre de manera tan hermosa que tuvo dos criaturas ahí abajo, en el río, porque no le daba tiempo a llegar a las casas, y ella misma las trajo en un pañal para que yo las arreglase.

YERMA.   ¿Y pudo venir andando desde el río?

DOLORES.   Vino. Con los zapatos y las enaguas empapadas en sangre…, pero con la cara reluciente.

YERMA.   ¿Y no le pasó nada?

DOLORES.   ¿Qué le iba a pasar? Dios es Dios.

YERMA.   Naturalmente. No le podía pasar nada, sino agarrar las criaturas y lavarlas con agua viva. Los animales los lamen,

---

[82] See Endnote **R**.

[83] This old woman (and her companion) are cronies of Dolores. The Vieja 1ª of Act 1 (who also appears in the play's final *cuadro*) is a completely different character.

[84] *I came to get what I'm after.* (See Endnote **S**).

73

¿verdad? A mí no me da asco de mi hijo. Yo tengo la idea de que las recién paridas están como iluminadas por dentro, y los niños se duermen horas y horas sobre ellas oyendo ese arroyo de leche tibia que les va llenando los pechos para que ellos mamen, para que ellos jueguen, hasta que no quieran más, hasta que retiren la cabeza – «otro poquito más, niño…» – y se les llene la cara y el pecho de gotas blancas.

DOLORES.	Ahora tendrás un hijo. Te lo puedo asegurar.

YERMA.	Lo tendré porque lo tengo que tener. O no entiendo el mundo. A veces, cuando ya estoy segura de que jamás, jamás…, me sube como una oleada de fuego por los pies y se me quedan vacías todas las cosas, y los hombres que andan por la calle y los toros y las piedras me parecen como cosas de algodón. Y me pregunto: ¿para qué estarán ahí puestos?[85]

VIEJA 1.ª	Está bien que una casada quiera hijos, pero si no los tiene, ¿por qué ese ansia de ellos? Lo importante de este mundo es dejarse llevar por los años. No te critico. Ya has visto cómo he ayudado a los rezos. Pero, ¿qué vega esperas dar a tu hijo, ni qué felicidad, ni qué silla de plata?[86]

YERMA.	Yo no pienso en el mañana; pienso en el hoy. Tú estás vieja y lo ves ya todo como un libro leído. Yo pienso que tengo sed y no tengo libertad. Yo quiero tener a mi hijo en los brazos para dormir tranquila y, óyelo bien y no te espantes de lo que digo: aunque yo supiera que mi hijo me iba a martirizar después y me iba a odiar y me iba a llevar de los cabellos por las calles, recibiría con gozo su nacimiento, porque es mucho mejor llorar por un hombre vivo que nos apuñala, que llorar por este fantasma sentado año tras año encima de mi corazón.

VIEJA 1.ª	Eres demasiado joven para oír consejo. Pero, mientras esperas la gracia de Dios, debes ampararte en el amor de tu marido.

[85] Yerma's perception of reality is structured by her hope for a child; when it fades, the world appears undifferentiated and insubstantial.

[86] The sense of the question seems to be 'How can you be sure your son will have wealth, happiness, high position?'

YERMA.   ¡Ay! Has puesto el dedo en la llaga más honda que tienen mis carnes.

DOLORES.   Tu marido es bueno.

YERMA. (*Se levanta.*)   ¡Es bueno! ¡Es bueno! ¿Y qué? Ojalá fuera malo. Pero no. Él va con sus ovejas por sus caminos y cuenta el dinero por las noches. Cuando me cubre,[87] cumple con su deber, pero yo le noto la cintura fría como si tuviera el cuerpo muerto, y yo, que siempre he tenido asco de las mujeres calientes, quisiera ser en aquel instante como una montaña de fuego.

DOLORES.   ¡Yerma!

YERMA.   No soy una casada indecente; pero yo sé que los hijos nacen del hombre y de la mujer. ¡Ay, si los pudiera tener yo sola!

DOLORES.   Piensa que tu marido también sufre.

YERMA.   No sufre. Lo que pasa es que él no ansía hijos.

VIEJA 1.ª   ¡No digas eso!

YERMA.   Se lo conozco en la mirada y, como no los ansía no me los da. No lo quiero, no lo quiero y, sin embargo, es mi única salvación.[88] Por honra y por casta. Mi única salvación.

VIEJA 1.ª (*Con miedo.*)   Pronto empezará a amanecer. Debes irte a tu casa.

DOLORES.   Antes de nada saldrán los rebaños y no conviene que te vean sola.

YERMA.   Necesitaba este desahogo.[89] ¿Cuántas veces repito las oraciones?

DOLORES.   La oración del laurel, dos veces, y al mediodía, la

---

[87] *Cover* (as stallions, rams or bulls do for breeding purposes). While it is a natural term for a country person to use, it does convey both Yerma's aggrieved suspicion that her husband regards her as part of his livestock, and her own assumption that sex is exclusively a means to procreation.

[88] See Endnote **T**.

[89] *I needed to get that off my chest.*

oración de Santa Ana.[90] Cuando te sientas encinta me traes la fanega de trigo que me has prometido.

VIEJA 1.ª   Por encima de los montes ya empieza a clarear. Vete.

DOLORES.   Como en seguida empezarán a abrir los portones, te vas dando un rodeo por la acequia.

YERMA. (*Con desaliento.*)   ¡No sé por qué he venido!

DOLORES.   ¿Te arrepientes?

YERMA.   ¡No!

DOLORES. (*Turbada.*)   Si tienes miedo, te acompañaré hasta la esquina

VIEJA 1.ª (*Con inquietud.*)   Van a ser las claras del día[91] cuando llegues a tu puerta.

(*Se oyen voces.*)

DOLORES.   ¡Calla ! (*Escuchan.*)

VIEJA 1.ª   No es nadie. Anda con Dios.

(YERMA *se dirige a la puerta y en este momento llaman a ella. Las tres mujeres quedan paradas.*)

DOLORES.   ¿Quién es?

VOZ   Soy yo.

YERMA.   Abre. (DOLORES *duda.*) ¿Abres o no?

(*Se oyen murmullos. Aparece* JUAN *con las dos* CUÑADAS.)

HERMANA 2.ª   Aquí está.

YERMA.   ¡Aquí estoy!

JUAN.   ¿Qué haces en este sitio? Si pudiera dar voces, levantaría a todo el pueblo, para que viera dónde iba la honra de mi casa; pero he de ahogarlo todo y callarme porque eres mi mujer.

YERMA.   Si pudiera dar voces, también las daría yo, para que se

---

[90] See Endnote **U**.
[91] *It will be bright daylight.*

levantaran hasta los muertos y vieran esta limpieza que me cubre.[92]

JUAN. ¡No, eso no ! Todo lo aguanto menos eso. Me engañas, me envuelves y, como soy un hombre que trabaja la tierra, no tengo ideas para tus astucias.

DOLORES. ¡Juan!

JUAN. ¡Vosotras, ni palabra!

DOLORES. (*Fuerte.*) Tu mujer no ha hecho nada malo.

JUAN. Lo está haciendo desde el mismo día de la boda. Mirándome con dos agujas, pasando las noches en vela con los ojos abiertos al lado mío, y llenando de malos suspiros mis almohadas.

YERMA. ¡Cállate!

JUAN. Y yo no puedo más. Porque se necesita ser de bronce[93] para ver a tu lado una mujer que te quiere meter los dedos dentro del corazón y que se sale de noche fuera de su casa, ¿en busca de qué? ¡Dime!, ¿buscando qué? Las calles están llenas de machos. En las calles no hay flores que cortar.[94]

YERMA. No te dejo hablar ni una sola palabra. Ni una más. Te figuras tú y tu gente que sois vosotros los únicos que guardáis honra, y no sabes que mi casta no ha tenido nunca nada que ocultar. Anda. Acércate a mí y huele mis vestidos, ¡acércate!, a ver dónde encuentras un olor que no sea tuyo, que no sea de tu cuerpo. Me pones desnuda en mitad de la plaza y me escupes. Haz conmigo lo que quieras, que soy tu mujer, pero guárdate de poner nombre de varón sobre mis pechos.

JUAN. No soy yo quien lo pone; lo pones tú con tu conducta y el pueblo lo empieza a decir. Lo empieza a decir claramente. Cuando llego a un corro, todos callan; cuando voy a pesar la harina, todos callan; y hasta de noche en el campo, cuando

---

[92] Yerma breaks into the traditional rhetoric of unjustly impugned honour.

[93] *You need to have no feelings at all.*

[94] *You don't go out on the street looking for flowers to pick.*

despierto, me parece que también se callan las ramas de los árboles.[95]

YERMA. Yo no sé por qué empiezan los malos aires que revuelcan al trigo y ¡mira tú si el trigo es bueno!

JUAN. Ni yo sé lo que busca una mujer a todas horas fuera de su tejado.

YERMA. (*En un arranque y abrazándose a su marido.*) Te busco a ti. Te busco a ti. Es a ti a quien busco día y noche sin encontrar sombra donde respirar. Es tu sangre y tu amparo lo que deseo.[96]

JUAN. Apártate.

YERMA. No me apartes y quiere conmigo.

JUAN. ¡Quita![97]

YERMA. Mira que me quedo sola. Como si la luna se buscara ella misma por el cielo. ¡Mírame! (*Lo mira.*)

JUAN. (*La mira y la aparta bruscamente.*) ¡Déjame ya de una vez!

DOLORES. ¡Juan!

(YERMA *cae al suelo.*)

YERMA. (*Alto.*) Cuando salía por mis claveles me tropecé con el muro. ¡Ay! ¡Ay! Es en ese muro donde tengo que estrellar mi cabeza.

JUAN. Calla. Vamos.

DOLORES. ¡Dios mío!

YERMA. (*A gritos.*) ¡Maldito sea mi padre, que me dejó su sangre de padre de cien hijos! ¡Maldita sea mi sangre, que los busca golpeando por las paredes!

JUAN. ¡Calla he dicho!

DOLORES. ¡Viene gente! Habla bajo.

---

[95] As it has for Yerma, the natural world has become for Juan a mirror of his own obsessions.

[96] See Endnote V.

[97] *Get away from me.*

78

YERMA.   No me importa. Dejarme libre siquiera la voz, ahora que voy entrando en lo más oscuro del pozo. (*Se levanta.*) Dejar que de mi cuerpo salga siquiera esta cosa hermosa y que llene el aire.

(*Se oyen voces.*)

DOLORES.   Van a pasar por aquí.

JUAN.   Silencio.

YERMA.   ¡Eso! ¡Eso! Silencio. Descuida.

JUAN.   Vamos. ¡Pronto!

YERMA.   ¡Ya está! ¡Ya está! ¡Y es inútil que me retuerza las manos! Una cosa es querer con la cabeza...

JUAN.   Calla.

YERMA. (*Bajo.*)   Una cosa es querer con la cabeza y otra cosa es que el cuerpo, maldito sea el cuerpo, no nos responda. Está escrito y no me voy a poner a luchar a brazo partido con los mares.[98] Ya está. ¡Que mi boca se quede muda! (*Sale.*)

Telón

CUADRO ÚLTIMO

Alrededores de una ermita en plena montaña.[99] *En primer término, unas ruedas de carro y unas mantas formando una tienda rústica, donde está* YERMA. *Entran las* MUJERES *con ofrendas a la ermita. Vienen descalzas. En la escena está la* VIEJA *alegre del primer acto.*[100]

(*Canto a telón corrido.*)

No te pude ver
cuando eras soltera,

---

[98] *It's my fate, and I'm not going to pit my strength against the force of the sea.*
[99] See Endnote **W**.
[100] i.e. the Vieja Pagana (so named in the list of *personajes*) with whom Yerma converses in the second *cuadro* of Act 1.

mas de casada te encontraré.
No te pude ver
cuando eras soltera.
Te desnudaré,
casada y romera,
cuando en lo oscuro las doce den.

VIEJA. (*Con sorna.*) ¿Habéis bebido ya el agua santa?

MUJER 1.ª Sí.

VIEJA. Y ahora, a ver a ése.[101]

MUJER 2.ª Creemos en él.

VIEJA. Venís a pedir hijos al santo y resulta que cada año vienen más hombres solos a esta romería. ¿Qué es lo que pasa? (*Ríe.*)

MUJER 1.ª ¿A qué vienes aquí, si no crees?

VIEJA. A ver. Yo me vuelvo loca por ver. Y a cuidar de mi hijo. El año pasado se mataron dos por una casada seca y quiero vigilar. Y, en último caso, vengo porque me da la gana.

MUJER 1.ª ¡Que Dios te perdone! (*Entran.*)

VIEJA. (*Con sarcasmo*) Que te perdone a ti.[102]

(*Se va. Entra* MARÍA *con la* MUCHACHA 1.ª)

MUCHACHA 1.ª ¿Y ha venido?

MARÍA. Ahí tienen el carro. Me costó mucho que vinieran.[103] Ella ha estado un mes sin levantarse de la silla. Le tengo miedo. Tiene una idea que no sé cuál es, pero desde luego es una idea mala.

MUCHACHA 1.ª Yo llegué con mi hermana. Lleva ocho años viniendo sin resultado.

MARÍA. Tiene hijos la que los tiene que tener.

MUCHACHA 1.ª Es lo que yo digo.

---

[101] i.e. the image of the miracle-working saint (substituted by Lorca for the portrait of Christ on a tapestry in the chapel at Moclín.)

[102] The Vieja Pagana neatly reminds the woman that the *romería* involves collusion in activities a christian would regard as sinful.

[103] *It was hard work getting them to come.*

(*Se oyen voces.*)

MARÍA.   Nunca me gustó esta romería. Vamos a las eras, que es donde está la gente.

MUCHACHA 1.ª   El año pasado, cuando se hizo oscuro, unos mozos atenazaron con sus manos los pechos de mi hermana.

MARÍA.   En cuatro leguas a la redonda no se oyen más que palabras terribles.[104]

MUCHACHA 1.ª   Más de cuarenta toneles de vino he visto en las espaldas de la ermita.

MARÍA.   Un río de hombres solos bajan por esas sierras.

(*Se oyen voces. Entra* YERMA *con seis mujeres que van a la iglesia. Van descalzas y llevan cirios rizados. Empieza el anochecer.*)

YERMA.
Señor, que florezca la rosa,
no me la dejéis en sombra.

MUJER 2.ª
Sobre su carne marchita
florezca la rosa amarilla.

YERMA.
Y en el vientre de tus siervas
la llama oscura de la tierra.

CORO DE MUJERES.
Señor, que florezca la rosa,
no me la dejéis en sombra.

(*Se arrodillan.*)

YERMA.
El cielo tiene jardines
con rosales de alegría:

---

[104] *for miles around all you hear is dreadful language.* Couples on their way to Moclín were traditionally the target of shouted allusions to the sexual activities that took place there.

entre rosal y rosal,
la rosa de maravilla.
Rayo de aurora parece
y un arcángel la vigila,
las alas como tormentas,
los ojos como agonías.
Alrededor de sus hojas
arroyos de leche tibia
juegan y mojan la cara
de las estrellas tranquilas.
Señor, abre tu rosal
sobre mi carne marchita.

(*Se levantan.*)

MUJER 2.ª

Señor, calma con tu mano
las ascuas de su mejilla.

YERMA.

Escucha a la penitente
de tu santa romería.
Abre tu rosa en mi carne
aunque tenga mil espinas.

CORO.

Señor, que florezca la rosa,
no me la dejéis en sombra.

YERMA.

Sobre mi carne marchita,
la rosa de maravilla.

(*Entran.*)

(*Salen* MUCHACHAS *corriendo con largas cintas en las manos, por la izquierda, y entran. Por la derecha, otras tres, con largas cintas y mirando hacia atrás, que entran también. Hay en la escena como un crescendo de voces, con ruidos de cascabeles y colleras de campanillas.*[105] *En un plano superior aparecen las*

---

[105] Instruments shaped like horse-collars with little bells attached to them.

82

siete MUCHACHAS, *que agitan las cintas hacia la izquierda. Crece el ruido y entran dos* MÁSCARAS *populares, una como macho y otra como hembra. Llevan grandes caretas. El* MACHO *empuña un cuerno de toro en la mano. No son grotescas de ningún modo, sino de gran belleza y con un sentido de pura tierra. La* HEMBRA *agita un collar de grandes cascabeles.*[106] *El fondo se llena de gente que grita y comenta la danza. Está muy anochecido.*)

NIÑO.   ¡El demonio y su mujer! ¡El demonio y su mujer!

HEMBRA.

En el río de la sierra
la esposa triste se bañaba.
Por el cuerpo le subían
los caracoles del agua.
La arena de las orillas
y el aire de la mañana
le daban fuego a su risa
y temblor a sus espaldas.
¡Ay qué desnuda estaba
la doncella en el agua!

NIÑO.

¡Ay cómo se quejaba!

HOMBRE 1.º

¡Ay marchita de amores
con el viento y el agua!

HOMBRE 2.º

¡Que diga a quién espera!

HOMBRE 1.º

¡Que diga a quién aguarda!

HOMBRE 2.º

¡Ay con el vientre seco
y la color quebrada!

[106] See Endnote **X**.

HEMBRA.

> Cuando llegue la noche lo diré,
> cuando llegue la noche clara.
> Cuando llegue la noche de la romería
> rasgaré los volantes de mi enagua.

CORO.

> Y en seguida vino la noche.
> ¡Ay, que la noche llegaba!
> Mirad qué oscuro se pone
> el chorro de la montaña.

(Empiezan a sonar unas guitarras.)

MACHO. (*Se levanta y agita el cuerno.*)

> ¡Ay qué blanca
> la triste casada!
> ¡Ay cómo se queja entre las ramas!
> Amapola y clavel serás luego,
> cuando el macho despliegue su capa.

(Se acerca.)

> Si tú vienes a la romería
> a pedir que tu vientre se abra,
> no te pongas un velo de luto,
> sino dulce camisa de holanda.
> Vete sola detrás de los muros,
> donde están las higueras cerradas,
> y soporta mi cuerpo de tierra
> hasta el blanco gemido del alba.
> ¡Ay, cómo relumbra!
> ¡Ay, cómo relumbraba!
> ¡Ay, cómo se cimbrea la casada!

HEMBRA.

> ¡Ay que el amor le pone
> coronas y guirnaldas,
> y dardos de oro vivo
> en sus pechos se clavan!

MACHO.

> Siete veces gemía,
> nueve se levantaba.
> Quince veces juntaron
> jazmines con naranjas.

HOMBRE 1.º

> ¡Dale ya con el cuerno![107]

HOMBRE 2.º

> Con la rosa y la danza.

HOMBRE 1.º

> ¡Ay cómo se cimbrea la casada!

MACHO.

> En esta romería
> el varón siempre manda.
> Los maridos son toros,[108]
> el varón siempre manda,
> y las romeras flores,
> para aquel que las gana.

NIÑO.

> Dale ya con el aire.

HOMBRE 2.º

> Dale ya con la rama.

MACHO.

> ¡Venid a ver la lumbre
> de la que se bañaba!

HOMBRE 1.º

> Como junco se curva.

NIÑO.

> Y como flor se cansa.

---

[107] *Let her have it with the horn!*.

[108] In the metaphorical language of cuckoldry the deceived husband is often represented as a bull, fierce and dangerous but easily deceived and subdued (as in a bull-fight) by daring and masterful men.

HOMBRES.

   ¡Que se aparten las niñas!

MACHO.

   ¡Que se queme la danza
   y el cuerpo reluciente
   de la limpia casada![109]

(*Se van bailando con son de palmas y música. Cantan.*)

   El cielo tiene jardines
   con rosales de alegría:
   entre rosal y rosal,
   la rosa de maravilla.

(*Vuelven a pasar dos* MUCHACHAS *gritando. Entra la* VIEJA *alegre.*)

VIEJA.   A ver si luego nos dejáis dormir. Pero luego será ella. (*Entra* YERMA.) ¿Tú?[110] (YERMA *está abatida y no habla.*) Dime: ¿para qué has venido?

YERMA.   No sé.

VIEJA.   ¿No te convences? ¿Y tu esposo?

(YERMA *da muestras de cansancio y de persona a la que una idea fija le oprime la cabeza.*)

YERMA.   Ahí está.

VIEJA.   ¿Qué hace?

YERMA.   Bebe. (*Pausa. Llevándose las manos a la frente.*) ¡Ay!

VIEJA.   ¡Ay, ay! Menos ¡ay! y más alma.[111] Antes no he querido decirte nada, pero ahora sí.

YERMA.   ¡Y qué me vas a decir que ya no sepa!

VIEJA.   Lo que ya no se puede callar. Lo que está puesto encima

---

[109] A clear invitation to scorch the purity of honour with the fire of lust.

[110] The Vieja Pagana is surprised that Yerma, who clings so fiercely to her honour, has come to an event which is really an opportunity for losing it.

[111] *stop moaning and show more spirit.*

86

del tejado.[112] La culpa es de tu marido, ¿Lo oyes? Me dejaría cortar las manos. Ni su padre, ni su abuelo, ni su bisabuelo se portaron como hombres de casta. Para tener un hijo ha sido necesario que se junte el cielo con la tierra. Están hechos con saliva.[113] En cambio, tu gente, no. Tienes hermanos y primos a cien leguas a la redonda. ¡Mira qué maldición ha venido a caer sobre tu hermosura!

YERMA.   Una maldición. Un charco de veneno sobre las espigas.[114]

VIEJA.   Pero tú tienes pies para marcharte de tu casa.

YERMA.   ¿Para marcharme?

VIEJA.   Cuando te vi en la romería me dio un vuelco el corazón.[115] Aquí vienen las mujeres a conocer hombres nuevos y el Santo hace el milagro. Mi hijo está sentado detrás de la ermita esperándome. Mi casa necesita una mujer. Vete con él y viviremos los tres juntos. Mi hijo sí es de sangre. Como yo. Si entras en mi casa, todavía queda olor de cunas. La ceniza de tu colcha se te volverá pan y sal para las crías. Anda. No te importe la gente. Y, en cuanto a tu marido, hay en mi casa entrañas y herramientas para que no cruce siquiera la calle.[116]

YERMA.   ¡Calla, calla! ¡Si no es eso! Nunca lo haría. Yo no puedo ir a buscar. ¿Te figuras que puedo conocer otro hombre? ¿Dónde pones mi honra? El agua no se puede volver atrás, ni la luna llena sale al mediodía. Vete. Por el camino que voy seguiré. ¿Has pensado en serio que yo me pueda doblar a otro hombre? ¿Que yo vaya a pedirle lo que es mío como una esclava? Conóceme, para que nunca me hables más. Yo no busco.

VIEJA.   Cuando se tiene sed, se agradece el agua.

YERMA.   Yo soy como un campo seco donde caben arando mil

---

[112] *It's plain for all to see.*

[113] *It took the sky falling on his head to make one of them beget a son. They're as weak as spittle.* (See Endnote **Y**).

[114] Yerma gloomily recapitulates the Vieja Pagana's comment on Juan at their first meeting.

[115] *my heart missed a beat.* (She felt a premonition.)

[116] *the will and weapons enough to stop him even showing his face.*

pares de bueyes, y lo que tú me das es un pequeño vaso de agua de pozo. Lo mío es dolor que ya no está en las carnes.

VIEJA. (*Fuerte*)   Pues sigue así. Por tu gusto es. Como los cardos del secano. Pinchosa,[117] marchita.

YERMA. (*Fuerte*)   Marchita sí, ¡ya lo sé! ¡Marchita! No es preciso que me lo refriegues por la boca. No vengas a solazarte, como los niños pequeños en la agonía de un animalito. Desde que me casé estoy dándole vueltas a esta palabra, pero es la primera vez que la oigo, la primera vez que me la dicen en la cara. La primera vez que veo que es verdad.

VIEJA.   No me das ninguna lástima,[118] ninguna. Yo buscaré otra mujer para mi hijo.

(*Se va. Se oye un gran coro lejano cantado por los romeros.* YERMA *se dirige hacia el carro y aparece por detrás del mismo su marido.*)

YERMA.   ¿Estabas ahí?

JUAN.   Estaba.

YERMA.   ¿Acechando?

JUAN.   Acechando.

YERMA.   ¿Y has oído?

JUAN.   Sí.

YERMA.   ¿Y qué? Déjame y vete a los cantos.[119] (*Se sienta en las mantas.*)

JUAN.   También es hora de que yo hable.

YERMA.   ¡Habla!

JUAN.   Y que me queje.

YERMA.   ¿Con qué motivo?

JUAN.   Que tengo el amargor en la garganta.

---

[117] *prickly* (dried out, unapproachable and 'inútil como un manojo de espinas', as Yerma has earlier described the lot of barren women).

[118] The Vieja Pagana has only scorn for what she regards as wilful stubbornness.

[119] *Go and join in the singing* (and drinking).

YERMA. Y yo en los huesos.

JUAN. Ha llegado el último minuto de resistir este continuo lamento por cosas oscuras, fuera de la vida, por cosas que están en el aire.

YERMA. (*Con asombro dramático.*) ¿Fuera de la vida dices? ¿En el aire dices?

JUAN. Por cosas que no han pasado y ni tú ni yo dirigimos.[120]

YERMA. (*Violenta.*) ¡Sigue! ¡Sigue!

JUAN. Por cosas que a mí no me importan. ¿Lo oyes? Que a mí no me importan. Ya es necesario que te lo diga. A mí me importa lo que tengo entre las manos. Lo que veo por mis ojos.

YERMA. (*Incorporándose de rodillas, desesperada.*) Así, así. Eso es lo que yo quería oír de tus labios. No se siente la verdad cuando está dentro de una misma, pero ¡qué grande y cómo grita cuando se pone fuera y levanta los brazos![121] ¡No le importa! ¡Ya lo he oído!

JUAN. (*Acercándose.*) Piensa que tenía que pasar así. Óyeme. (*La abraza para incorporarla.*) Muchas mujeres serían felices de llevar tu vida. Sin hijos es la vida más dulce. Yo soy feliz no teniéndolos. No tenemos culpa ninguna.

YERMA. ¿Y qué buscabas en mí?

JUAN A ti misma.

YERMA. (*Excitada.*) ¡Eso! Buscabas la casa, la tranquilidad y una mujer. Pero nada más. ¿Es verdad lo que digo?

JUAN. Es verdad. Como todos.

YERMA. ¿Y lo demás? ¿Y tu hijo?

JUAN. (*Fuerte.*) ¡No oyes que no me importa! ¡No me preguntes más! ¡Que te lo tengo que gritar al oído para que lo sepas, a ver si de una vez vives ya tranquila!

---

[120] *which neither of us have any control over.*

[121] Yerma echoes her perception (during her final interview with Víctor) of the transfiguring force of suppressed feelings when unleashed through open expression.

YERMA. ¿Y nunca has pensado en él cuando me has visto desearlo?

JUAN. Nunca.

(*Están los dos en el suelo.*)

YERMA. ¿Y no podré esperarlo?

JUAN. No.

YERMA. ¿Ni tú?

JUAN. Ni yo tampoco. ¡Resígnate!

YERMA. ¡Marchita!

JUAN. Y a vivir en paz. Uno y otro, con suavidad, con agrado. ¡Abrázame! (*La abraza.*)

YERMA, ¿Qué buscas?

JUAN. A ti te busco.[122] Con la luna estás hermosa.

YERMA. Me buscas como cuando te quieres comer una paloma.

JUAN. Bésame… así.

YERMA. Eso nunca. Nunca. (YERMA *da un grito y aprieta la garganta de su esposo. Éste cae hacia atras.* YERMA *le aprieta la garganta hasta matarle. Empieza el coro de la romería.*) Marchita, marchita, pero segura. Ahora sí que lo sé de cierto. Y sola. (*Se levanta. Empieza a llegar gente.*) Voy a descansar sin despertarme sobresaltada, para ver si la sangre me anuncia otra sangre nueva.[123] Con el cuerpo seco para siempre. ¿Qué queréis saber? No os acerquéis, porque he matado a mi hijo. ¡Yo misma he matado a mi hijo!

(*Acude un grupo que queda parado al fondo. Se oye el coro de la romería.*)

Telón

[122] Juan's words recall Yerma's in the previous scene, but he means something very different. Yerma was looking for the 'Juan who could be'. He, however, shows he is content with her 'as she is', simply as an agreeable object in his conveniently arranged world.
[123] *without waking with a start, anxious to see if I feel new life in my blood.*

Endnotes

A What is indicated by the stage directions 'entra' and 'sale' is not invariably clear in *Yerma* (both exits and entrances can be indicated by either term). But 'cuando sale el pastor', unlike the preceding 'un pastor sale de puntillas', evidently refers to the shepherd *leaving* the stage, thus marking the end of Yerma's dream and a return to conscious reality ('una alegre luz de mañana'). The careful indications of movement and lighting for the dumb show with which the play opens, combined with the evocative use of traditional song, immediately alert us to the way important meanings can be conveyed by elements outside the spoken dialogue as well as within it. Even before Yerma speaks the audience senses her obsessive yearning, and is thus well able to catch the underlying drift of her opening exchanges with her husband, as well as being prepared for the intensity of her inner reveries later in the scene, as she accompanies her rhythmical sewing with a verse dialogue with an imaginary child.

B Yerma moves abruptly to a mode of expression which, through its lack of practical relevance, directs attention to underlying symbolic meanings. Indeed, she articulates here one of the central motifs of the play: the vivifying power of the elements, especially flowing water, which can only take effect outside the inhibitive confines of the house. While such directness and economy of means is a feature of the play's dramatic style, it can also serve to emphasize the way Yerma's single-minded preoccupation is reflected in her compulsive talk.

C Yerma gloomily adapts Juan's moralizing dictum, pointing out that she *is* someone with nothing better to do. Yerma frequently contests the validity of standard moral definitions, especially those which constrain the scope of women's lives, but it is more the protest of a wronged outcast from the fold than that of a rebel seeking to reject constraints. Nevertheless, her propensity to echo ironically the language of such definitions does draw attention both to their function as a form of social control and her own strong sense of her worth as an individual.

D Víctor's jocular rustic metaphor can also refer to mental concentration or application. Thus the related issues of Juan's perfunctory sexual performance and his failure to appreciate the intensity of his wife's longing are combined. Lorca cited this comment as one example of his aim to create a dramatic language which simultaneously expressed two levels of meaning. (*Conv.*, 42).

E Yerma seems to have a penchant for pain, (she has already described the pain of chilbirth as 'un dolor fresco, bueno'), as if physical suffering were a way of earning happiness, whereas straightforward sensual enjoyment is regarded as shameful. As she tells the Vieja Pagana, in the next scene, it is 'nunca por divertirme' that she gives her body to her husband; what she hopes for is 'un hijo que sufrir' (2, 2).

F The recurrent theme of verbal taboos is apparent here, but, at the same time, we should note that the Vieja Pagana has made her opinions and advice adequately clear to anyone with ears to hear. Incomprehension such as Yerma's, she realizes, is the blindness of obsession and strong inhibitions rather than mere ingenuousness. The old woman's tactics (emphasizing Yerma's physical attractiveness and the pleasurable fulfilment it deserves, making her recall feelings for another man, and hinting, by over-protesting rules of honour, that there are ways and means to infringe them) could put audiences in mind of the go-betweens and underminers of virtue sometimes found in Spanish dramas of adultery and revenge, whose remote literary antecedent is La Celestina. This episode would seem to be one of the moments, mentioned by Lorca, in which the impression is given of a conventional intrigue developing.

G This rather contrived and portentous statement can perhaps be understood as an attempt by the Vieja Pagana to assert that a husband who is infertile is morally detestable (and thus unworthy of fidelity). The statement also confirms her 'pagan' view of things. The only role she can envisage for a vengeful deity is that of exterminating those perverse beings who, in her view, seek to thwart the spontaneous joy and fecundity of creation.

H Such attacks on children did occasionally occur in rural areas. Lorca told Pablo Neruda, in 1934, that he had been profoundly shocked to witness pigs attack and devour a lamb in a rural area visited by *La Barraca*, (See Pablo Neruda, *Memoirs*, trans. Hardie St Martin (London: Souvenir Press, 1977), 123-4.

I Although the Second Girl contributes little to the play's action, Yerma's exchanges with her here have considerable structural importance. The girl's non-conformist contentment with childlessness not only contrasts strongly with Yerma's unhappy exclusion from what she sees as her life's purpose, but also serves to put a whole set of traditional attitudes into critical perspective. The dialogue also prepares the ground for the last two scenes of the play, Yerma's visit to Dolores the 'wise woman' (the Second Girl's mother), and the pilgrimage to the shrine of the miracle-working *santo*. The evident failure of Dolores to remedy her own daughter's childlessness is in no way inconsistent (as some critics have suggested) with Yerma's subsequent recourse to her services. Rather it is a further example of Lorca's insight into his protagonist's state of mind. People driven to superstition are notoriously impervious to rational evidence of its inefficacy, preferring to ascribe such failures to some contamination of the magic (in this instance, the girl's not wanting a child, a negative attitude to which, in the case of her own husband, Yerma readily attributes contraceptive effectiveness).

J Víctor, like the Vieja Pagana, although possibly less consciously, senses the danger-ous force of Yerma's emotions. The action of averting his eyes suggests a failure to sustain the potent gaze of the shepherd in Yerma's initial dream, itself brought to mind by the device of Yerma taking up – with intense feeling – the traditional love-song addressed to a shepherd which Víctor had been singing. In terms of the minimal conventional intrigue, it is established here that there will now be no illicit relationship. The opportunity has come and gone, the challenging invitation has been decisively turned down. Henceforth Yerma will be the victim of suspicions that are unjustified as far as her actual behaviour is concerned.

K Water for irrigation is often controlled simply by opening or blocking up outlets in the channel. If Juan were robbed of water during his allotted turn, the thieves would be his farmer neighbours. Juan's underlying motivation is the need he feels to protect what is exclusively his against the depradations of an opportunistic community, whether the source of his worry is the possible access of others to his crops, his wife or his reputation (i.e. through gossip). Among several levels of irony here, it is worth noting that it is precisely Juan's determination to guard the purely utilitarian value of 'his' water that deprives Yerma, confined in the house, of the emotional fulfilment which water so insistently symbolizes in the play.

92

L The careful arrangement of the figures for this choral sequence shows Lorca's concern to achieve a strong visual impact, reinforcing the counterpointing of different voices and the alternation of song, prose dialogue and rhythmically chanted verse. The contrast of black and white, for instance, between clothes worn and garments being washed, forcefully suggests the elemental tensions between fecundity and barrenness, sexuality and moral laws, callousness and compassion which the chatter and songs of the women bring out in detail. The initial inspiration for this remarkable scene may have come from a visit Lorca made to Cáñar, nestled high on a southern slope of the Sierra Nevada. In 1926 he wrote to his brother that he would never forget the village, 'lleno de lavanderas cantando y pastores sombríos' (808).

M The malicious term 'machorra' denotes a barren female animal, but might also suggest masculine traits (presumably because Yerma does not keep to the submissive reclusion of women's domestic activities). It can be compared with Yerma's own 'ojalá fuera yo una mujer' at the end of the previous scene. Her criticized actions confirm her unconscious urge to be in physical contact with life-giving natural elements.

N The accusation that Yerma carries an image (a 'portrait') of Víctor in her eyes seems to be based on the traditional notion of the eyes as windows of the soul; the laundress's comments provide one of the most striking examples, among a number in the play, of the importance of 'la mirada', both in the significance of holding or avoiding eye-contact, and as an indication of feelings which cannot – or must not – be put into words.

O This is the only occasion we see Juan not confronting Yerma, and shows him in a slightly more sympathetic light. His obsession with work and financial security brings him no happiness, and his comment on the apple, while it calls to mind his failure to fulfil her hopes as a bride ('cómo huelen a manzanas estas ropas'), belies Yerma's remarks on men's unappreciative, practical outlook later in the scene. The way he immediately qualifies his laying down the law about honour shows he is, as he later admits, unable to play the fiercely dominant role expected of husbands with conviction, in keeping with a code that equates considerateness or tolerance with weakness.

P These words provide a powerfully succinct revelation of Yerma's uncompromising outlook. In getting married she had made an irrevocable personal contract, exchanging her freedom for the satisfaction of her maternal urge. Cheated of this fulfilment, it is not merely that she will not give up hope: she proudly refuses to forgo what she regards as her rights, and her whole life has become a demand for justice that only death can make her relinquish.

Q The care with which the protagonist's name has been avoided in the dialogue so far has been in preparation for this moment. As she slips away into the darkening world, her identity is repeatedly uttered, like an accusation, by figures whose previous silence gives the naming an ominously oracular force. All Yerma's efforts are futile, she may temporarily escape the vigilant household, but she will never escape her fate.

R Dolores practises as a 'wise woman', or healer, offering a variety of services and methods, ranging from empirical expertise (herbs and potions) to incantations and prayers. Juan's eventual reaction to finding Yerma in Dolores' house might suggest her services to women are not invariably above-board, or are, at least, viewed with suspicion.

S Yerma is so dedicated to her single objective that she is completely inured to unpleasant features of the means of attaining it. She confronts the frightening darkness of the graveyard as resolutely as she endures the constraints of marriage and the distasteful necessity of sexual intimacy.

T The contradictory nature of Yerma's beliefs and feelings are becoming increasingly evident. Not only does she oscillate wildly between optimism and despair, but she also accuses her husband of being cold while she herself regards physical responsiveness with some repugnance, and of not desiring her happiness while admitting she does not love him. In a sense, Yerma has transferred her own inner tensions to Juan, while her inhibitive self-esteem, her traditional sense of *honra*, obliges her to define him as the exclusive agent of the emotional needs she fiercely defends as deeply-rooted in her own being.

U An eighteenth century example of such an 'oración' begins

      Santa Ana parió a la Virgen,

      la Virgen a mi Señor Jesucristo

thus making explicit the significance of this saint as a potent progenitor. (See Mª-Helena Sánchez Ortega, *La mujer y la sexualidad en el antiguo régimen* (Madrid: Akal, 1991, 275.)

V Although there seems to be a contradiction here with Yerma's previous expressions of resentment and lack of love for Juan, we should realize that she has now gone past the point where her motives and meanings can be assessed by narrowly rational criteria. In attempting to express an obscure truth of her feelings, she is possibly attributing to Juan the same alienated incompleteness she is so painfully aware of in herself. Since there can be no other man for her, she needs to believe in the possibility that, through her hoping and striving, her present, unsatisfactory partner could turn into the 'real' Juan, the husband and father she could love, desire and respect.

W The setting for this scene is inspired by Moclín, a rocky hill-top village to the north of Granada, and the site of a pilgrimage every October to the shrine of 'El Cristo del Paño', an image believed to have the power to make barren women fertile. Lorca had earlier collaborated on a ballet, *La romería de los cornudos* (the Cuckolds' Pilgrimage), a work with the same setting as this final scene, and the same underlying assumption that pregnancy was more likely to result from opportunities for sexual encounters with young men during the rites, celebrations and drinking, than from any miraculous powers possessed by the object of the pilgrims' veneration. (See GIBSON, 2, 247-251.)

X According to Lorca's brother, the apparel of the two figures is based on a folk dance of Asturias, although the masks are Lorca's addition (see FRANCISO GARCÍA LORCA, 1989, 218). The intention is to suggest an ancient ritual kept alive under the cloak of popular Christian beliefs and ceremonies.

Y The Vieja Pagana seems to be conflating two uses of the expression 'heaven and earth': to make a huge effort (*mover cielo y tierra*) and to panic in a tight spot (*juntársele a uno el cielo con la tierra*). The evocatively condensed use of popular expressions is a feature of the play's language in general.

Temas de discusión

Acto primero, cuadro 1

1. Estudia las acotaciones a lo largo de este cuadro. ¿Hasta qué punto los efectos que describen nos ayudan a comprender los motivos y preocupaciones de Yerma?
2. ¿Qué idea se nos da en este cuadro de la personalidad de Juan?
3. Analiza los comentarios de Yerma sobre la maternidad. ¿Por qué será que ella parece entender tanto de este asunto?
4. Cuando Víctor dice 'si es niña le pondrás tu nombre', ¿a qué se refiere el pastor, y por qué reacciona Yerma con tanta agitación?

Acto primero, cuadro 2

5. Analiza los comentarios de Yerma, y los de los otros personajes que salen en este cuadro, sobre el tema estar en/estar fuera de casa. ¿Qué diferencias de opinión notas?
6. La Vieja 1.ª se denomina (en otras ocasiones) 'vieja alegre' y 'vieja pagana'. A juzgar por su intervención en este cuadro, ¿están justificados estos apodos?
7. ¿En qué consiste 'la locura' de la Muchacha 2.ª?
8. Es la segunda vez que vemos a Yerma a solas con Víctor. ¿Crees que sus profundos sentimientos son inconscientes, o que ella no se atreve a reconocerlos abiertamente? Y él, ¿qué siente?

Acto segundo, cuadro 1

9. ¿Qué información nos transmite este cuadro sobre la situación doméstica de Juan y Yerma?
10. A los ojos de las lavanderas, ¿cuál es el 'pecado' más grave de Yerma: ser estéril o desear a otro hombre?
11. Juan y sus dos hermanas también son objeto de escarnio. ¿Por qué?
12. Analiza los principales símbolos que aparecen en los versos que celebran la fecundidad?

Acto segundo, cuadro 2

13. Las hermanas de Juan no pronuncian ni una palabra hasta el final del cuadro. Entonces, ¿cómo contribuye su presencia al desarrollo del mismo?
14. La cena familiar es, generalmente, una ocasión de feliz convivencia. ¿Y aquí?
15. Se nota una falta de mutua comprensión entre Juan y Yerma. ¿Cuáles son los principales motivos de su incompatibilidad?
16. Compara la estructura de este cuadro con la del primer cuadro de la obra. ¿Cuáles son las diferencias más importantes?
17. ¿Cómo interpretas el diálogo entre Yerma y Víctor, y qué significa para ella la partida definitiva del pastor?

Acto tercero, cuadro 1

18. ¿Cómo imaginas el cementerio donde Yerma ha estado con Dolores?
19. Dolores dice 'Ahora tendrás un niño. Te lo aseguro'. ¿Qué motivos tiene para hacer tal afirmación?
20. A juzgar por sus declaraciones anteriores a la llegada de Juan, ¿te parece Yerma una persona resuelta o más bien obsesiva?
21. ¿Te parece injusta la reacción de Juan al descubrir a su esposa en casa de Dolores? Describe lo que pasa en la parte final del cuadro desde el punto de vista del marido.

Acto tercero, cuadro 2

22. En cuanto invocaciones a la fertilidad, ¿qué diferencias de perspectiva y tono encuentras entre los versos de Yerma y los del Macho y la Hembra?
23. ¿Cómo se consigue el contraste entre la animación de la muchedumbre y el abatimiento de Yerma?
24. ¿Cuál es la solución que propone la Vieja para el problema de Yerma? ¿Te extraña que Yerma la rechace tan rotundamente?
25. Las palabras finales de Yerma, 'yo misma he matado a mi hijo', ¿qué interpretación les das?

96

Temas de disertación:

1. Se oyen canciones de tipo tradicional en cuatro de los seis cuadros de *Yerma*. (1,1; 1,2; 2,1; 3,2.). Estudia la función dramática de estas canciones.

2. ¿Cómo se indica el transcurso del tiempo en la obra, y qué trascendencia tiene este tema?

3. ¿Qué concepto del honor defiende Yerma? – ¿Y Juan?

4. 'Igual que Yerma, Juan se siente ofendido y humillado por la conducta y la postura de su cónyuge'. ¿Te parece acertado este comentario?

5. ¿Qué importancia tienen los siguientes personajes para el desarrollo de la acción: Víctor; María; la Vieja Pagana.

6. El acto de violencia que cierra la obra, ¿es un final fácil o corresponde a una lógica interna?

7. Analiza, en el lenguaje de *Yerma*, el contraste entre los símbolos de la fertilidad (el agua, las flores, etc.) y los de la esterilidad (la tierra seca, la roca, etc.).

8. 'A excepción de Yerma, no hay personajes bien definidos ni desarrollados'. ¿Estás de acuerdo con esta afirmación?

9. ¿Siguen produciéndose en nuestra sociedad los problemas que acosan a Yerma?

10. ¿Hasta qué punto se puede afirmar que *Yerma* encarna una crítica a la subordinación de la mujer en la sociedad tradicional?

Selected vocabulary

The following have been in general omitted from the vocabulary:

1. words that a sixth-form student can reasonably be expected to know with all textually-relevant meanings (e.g. **levantar**, *to raise*; **-se**, *to get up*; **llevar**, *to take / wear*; but NOT **madroño**, *bobble*; **sentir**, *to feel sorry / hear*).

2. words that are similar in form and relevant meaning to the English (e.g. **carácter**, *character*, *personality*; but NOT **doctora**, *wise woman*).

3. words that are dealt with in footnotes or endnotes.

The meanings given are those that are most helpful for understanding the sense in the relevant context. Asterisked words are not in the text of *Yerma* but appear in the introduction or notes.

abatido, depressed
ablandar, to soften
*abocar, to lead towards
abrazar, embrace
acá, here
acechar, to spy on
aceite, oil / olive oil
acentuarse, to become more intense
acequia, irrigation channel
acero, steel
*acomodado, well off
acudir, to approach
*achabacanar, to coarsen
achaque, fixed idea
adelfa, oleander
adiós, hello / goodbye
*adormecer, to lull to sleep
adormilado, dozing
agarrar, to seize
agradecer, to thank
agrado, pleasure
aguantar, to bear / put up with
aguardar, to wait for
aguja, needle

ahogado, muffled / choking with emotion
ahogar, to stifle / choke
alacena, cupboard
algazara, hubbub
algodón, cotton wool
alhelí, wallflower
*aliento, breath / stimulus
aligerar, to hurry
aliviar, to soothe
almohada, pillow
*alpargata, espadrille (typical workman's footwear)
alzar, to raise
amapola, poppy
amargo, bitter; **amargor**, bitterness
amarrado, tied
ampararse, find support
amparo, protection, help
anís, aniseed (-flavoured drink)
anochecido, dark
ansiar, to long for
apartar, to push away; **-se**, to go away
apretar, to grip

apuntar, to sprout
apuñalar, to stab
arado, plough
arañazo, scratch
arar, to plough
arramblar, to sweep aside
*arrancar, to rip out
arranque, sudden impulse
arrayán, myrtle
arrepentirse, to repent / regret
arroyo, stream
arrugado, wrinkled
asco, disgust; tener - de, be disgusted by
ascuas, glowing embers
asomarse, to look out
asombro, astonishment
astucia, slyness
atardecer, dusk
ataúd, coffin
atenazar, to grip / squeeze
*atravesar, to cross
aturdido, bewildered
aurora, dawn
ave, bird
avispa, wasp

bañarse, to bathe
*bienaventurado, happy
bisabuelo, great-grandfather
blanquear, whiten / whitewash
boda, wedding
bordar, to embroider
bostezo, yawn
boyero, oxherd
buey, ox
*butacas, front stalls (theatre)

cabellos, hair
caber, to fit into, have enough room
calar, soak / get wet
calceta, knitting
caliente, hot, randy
cáliz, calyx / cup
callar, to be quiet / not speak
camisa, shirt / shift
campanilla, little bell
canasto, basket
cántaro, pitcher
capa, cloak

capricho, whim, fancy
*captar, to understand, appreciate
caracol, sea-shell / whorl
caracola, conch /horn
cardo, thistle
careta, mask
carne (s), flesh
carrasposo, hoarse /harsh
carro, cart
cascabel, little bell
casta, caste / ancestry
*castigar, to condemn, punish
ceniza, ash
cerdo, pig
cesta, basket
ciervo, stag
cigarra, cricket, cicada
cimbrear, sway / move gracefully
cinta, ribbon
cintura, waist
cirio, candle
clarear, to become light
clavarse, to pierce, stick in
clavel, carnation
clavo, nail
cobertizo, shed
cobres, copper-ware
colcha, mattress
colmado, abundant
colorete, rouge
collar, collar, metal ring
cómplice, with complicity, pretending
confitura, jam / fruit preserve
conformidad, agreement /acquiescence
consejo, advice
*cónyuge, spouse
cordero, lamb
coro, chorus
corro, group of people
cortinita, lace curtain
coser, to sew
costura, sewing
cresta, summit
cría, having children / child
criar, to raise (children); -se, to be
    brought up
criatura, child / girl; crío, child
cuadro, scene
cuerno, horn

cuidar, to look after
culpa, blame
cuna, cradle
cuñada, sister-in-law
charco, pool of water
chico, tiny
chocita, little hut
chorro, gush of water

dar la gana, to feel like doing
dar vueltas, turn over (in the mind)
dardo, dart
delantal, apron
dentro, off-stage
desahogarse, recover, gain relief
desahogo, relief
descalzo, barefoot
descuidar, to not worry
*desequilibrio, lack of balance
deshacer, to disarrange
deslizarse por, to slip into; * to follow
   without difficulty
desnudar to undress
desocupado, idle
despegar, to open
desplegar, to unfold
desviar, to turn aside
dirigir, to control; - **la conversación** to
   speak to; **-se a,** to go up to
doblarse, to bow down
doctora, wise woman
doncella, girl
dueño, owner

embozo, turndown (of a sheet)
empeñarse, to insist
empuñar, to brandish
enaguas, petticoats
encaje, lace
encargado, given the job of
encharcar, to swamp
endulzar, to sweeten
engañador, deceitful
enjundia, grease
enjuto, thin
ensartar, to skewer
enseñanza, teaching
enterado, knowledgeable
enterarse, to find out

entrar, enter OR exit (in stage directions)
entregarse, to give oneself
envolver, implicate / confuse
*equívoco, equivocal, mistaken
era, threshing-floor / field
erguirse, to straighten / stand up
ermita, hermitage
escarcha, frost
esclavo, slave
escrito, destined
escupir, to spit
espalda, slope / mountainside
espantarse, to be alarmed
espesura, thicket / dense part
esquila, sheep-bell
esquina, street corner
estrellar, to shatter

faena, work / task
falda, skirt
fanega, measure of wheat (1 bushel)
fango, mud
fantasma, ghost
feo, unseemly
feria, fair
figuración, imagining
figurarse, to imagine
fingido, dissembling
flechado, irresistibly attracted
fondo, depths / back
fregar, to scrub
fundir, to melt

*gallinero, upper gallery, 'gods'
   (theatre)
ganado, flock
garganta, throat
gemir, to moan / sigh
golpe, blow
golpear, to beat
gota, droplet
grieta, fissure
guardar, to hold
guirnalda, garland
guisar, to cook
guiso, stew

hacienda, farm(lands)
harina, flour

helar, to freeze
hembra, female
herramienta, implement / weapon
higuera, fig tree
hilo, linen
holanda, fine linen
hormiga, ant
***hosco**, grim
hueso, bone

ilusión, high hopes
incorporarse, to straighten up
infamia, scandal / disgrace
infierno, hell
intención, hinted meaning
inundación, flood

jaramago, hedge mustard
junco, rush / reed
juntar, amass / join

labor, farm work
lagarto, lizard
lamer, to lick
lana, wool
lástima, pity
latir, to shake / pulse
lavandera, washerwoman
lejano, distant
lengua, tongue
licencia, permission
lindo, pretty
lío, bundle
lucha, struggle
lumbre, light
luto, mourning / black

llaga, wound
llano, plain

machacado, crushed
macho, male
machorra, barren female animal /
    masculine woman
madroño, bobble, tassel
maldición, curse
maldito, cursed
mamar, to suckle
manantial, spring(water)

manojo, handful
manta, blanket
mantel, tablecloth
mantón, shawl
marchito, withered
martillo, hammer
martirizar, to torment
máscara, masked performer
***materializado**, materialistic
mejilla, cheek
mendicante, beggar
molino, mill
***morbo**, disease
mortaja, shroud
mudo, dumb
mugir, to low (oxen)
murmurador, gossip-mongering
muro, wall
muslo, thigh

nacimiento, birth
nana, lullaby
nave, ship
nevada, patch of snow
novia, bride
novio, sweetheart
nuca, nape of neck

ofrenda, votive offering
oleada, wave
oler a, to smell of
ombligo, navel
oprimir, weigh down
oración, incantation, prayer
orilla, bank / shore
oveja, sheep

***palco**, box (theatre)
paloma/o, dove
pan tierno, soft / fresh bread
pañal, nappy
paños, clothes
parado, motionless
***paraíso**, upper gallery, 'gods' (theatre)
parir, to give birth
pasto, pasture
pastor, shepherd
patio, yard; * - **de butacas**, stalls
    (theatre)

pecado, sin
pechos, breasts
pedernal, flint
pegado, stuck
penumbra, dusk, semi-darkness
pesar, to weigh
pisar, to step
planchado, ironed
plano, level
plata, silver
*platea, front stalls (theatre)
podar, to prune
*podredumbre, rottenness
podrido, rotten
polvos, face-powder
portarse, to behave
portón, main door
*pote, jar, pot
pozo, well
prado, meadow
prenderse, to wear (adornments)
primeriza, primer (woman having first child)
primo, cousin
privar, withhold / deprive
propósito, a suitable
puerto, mountain pass
pujante, powerful
pulso, (heart)beat
puntillas, de on tiptoe
*puñalada, grievous blow

quejarse, to complain
quejumbroso, querulous
quemadura, sunburn
quemar, to burn /scorch

ramo, bunch / branch
rasgar, to tear
rayo, lightning
realizar, to achieve
rebajado, demeaned
recién parida, woman who has just given birth
recoger, to collect
redil, sheep pen
refregar, to rub hard, scrub
refresco, cool drink
regar, to water

relinchar, whinny
relumbrar, to shine
remero, oarsman
requesón, curds / cottage cheese
*resuelto, solved (problem, difficulty)
retama, broom
retorcer, twist; - las manos, wring one's hands
retratado, pictured
revolcar, to crush /blight
rezo, prayer
risa, laugh(ter)
rizado, curly / fluted
rizar, to ruffle
roble, oak
rocío, dew
rodear, to trim (with lace)
rodeo, detour
rodillas, de kneeling
rogar, to beg for
*romance, ballad
romería, pilgrimage
romero, pilgrim
ropas, bed-clothes
rosal, rosebush

sábana, sheet
sal, salt
secano, dry piece of land
segador, reaper
seguir, to continue
seguro, certain / safe
sentir, to feel (sorry) / hear
señalar, to point at
*señoritos, aristos, idle rich
siervo, servant
sigilosamente, furtively
simiente, seed
sino, fate
sobresaltado, startled
solazarse, to take pleasure
solería, flooring
soltera, unmarried woman.
sombrío, gloomy
sonar, to make a sound; (teeth) to chatter
sorbo, sip
sordo, deaf
sorna, sarcasm

sosegado, tranquil
suspiro, sigh

tabaque de costura, sewing basket
tajada, slice
tallo, stem
tapar, to cover / hide
techo, ceiling
tela, cloth
telón, curtain; a - corrido, with the
   curtains closed
temblar, to tremble
tibio, warm
tijeras, scissors
tirar, to pull
tomillo, thyme
tonel, barrel
torcido, twisted
torito, bull-calf
torrente, mountain stream
torta, cake / tart
trajecitos, baby clothes
tranco, threshold
transcurrir, to pass
trenza, braid (hair)
tropezarse con, to run into
tumba, grave

untar, to smear
vacío, empty / barren
vaho, breath
vara, yard (of cloth)
varón, man / male
vecino, neighbour
vega, fertile lowland
vela, en awake
velo, veil
velón, oil-lamp
veneno, poison
vidrio, shard of glass
vientre, belly
vigilar, to watch over
vivienda, dwelling
voces, shouts
volante, ruffle
voluntad, sin weak-willed
volverse, to become / turn around

yerbajos, unpleasant-tasting herbs
yerto, stiff
yunta, pair of oxen

zagal, shepherd boy
zagalón, grown lad